P9-CKO-743

THE
SOUTHERN
LADY

Arthur Mann
Advisory Editor in American History

Anne Firor Scott

The University of Chicago Press
Chicago and London

THE
SOUTHERN
LADY,

*From
Pedestal
to Politics
1830-1930*

$3.95 Pub. 3-11-81 (Quemori)

The University of Chicago Press, Chicago 60637
The University of Chicago Press, Ltd., London

81 80 79 78 77   9876543

International Standard Book Number: 0–226–74346–2 (clothbound)
Library of Congress Catalog Card Number: 73–123750

For A. M. S.
Sine te nihil

Contents

Preface

This study began with the discovery of a paradox. Some years ago I sought to delineate certain aspects of the progressive movement in the South. Time after time records of political reform movements revealed the presence of a woman or of a group of women who had played a significant role, and this before women were enfranchised. As a southerner I knew, or thought I knew, that "woman's place" was not in the political arena; yet there she was, active and effective. The effort to explain how this could be has led me down a long road. The discrepancy between appearance and reality in the progressive period made me wonder how much of what I thought I knew about earlier southern women, those fabled antebellum ladies, was also wrong. I was led to wonder, too, what had happened in the first years after women gained the right to vote. Did the women who had been so effective without the vote go on to significant accomplishment once they were enfranchised?

When I looked at the problem backward and forward, the paradox of the progressive women began to disappear. I came to understand that southern women in the years before 1860 had been the subjects—perhaps the victims—of an image of woman which was at odds with the reality of their lives. This image was weakened but not destroyed by the experiences of the Civil War and Reconstruction. It continued to shape the behavior of southern women for many years and has never entirely disappeared. For this reason women in the progressive period carefully cherished a ladylike aspect and were modest about their achievements. The power of the image also helped to explain the kinds of women who appeared in southern reform movements: those of impeccable antecedents and secure family position.

This book does not attempt to be a comprehensive history of southern women. Its purpose is fourfold: to describe the culturally defined image of the lady; to trace the effect this definition had on women's behavior; to describe the realities of women's lives which were often at odds with the image; to describe and characterize the struggle of women to free themselves from the confines of cultural expectation and find a way to self-determination.

Such a study could be made of American women in general, for the idea of the lady was part of the larger American and even Anglo-American culture of the nineteenth century. Southern women were a particularly interesting part of the whole, however, because in the South the image of the lady took deep root and had far-reaching social consequences. The social role of women was unusually confining there, and the sanctions used to enforce obedience peculiarly effective. One result was that southern women became in time a distinct type among American women. Another was that their efforts to free themselves were more complex than those of women elsewhere.

This book deals largely with women who left a mark on the historical record, which means for the most part women of educated or wealthy families. In antebellum times the wives of small farmers and the slave women lived, bore children, worked hard, and died, leaving little trace for the historian coming after. Such women were not much affected by role expectations. When they sweated in the fields or tore their hands digging in the ground no one lectured them on feminine delicacy or told them it was unladylike to work so long and hard. In more recent times, too, definitions of what was ladylike were reserved for women of the elite group, not for wives of mill workers or Negro maids.

Everybody knows that the South is immensely varied, that Louisiana is different from North Carolina, and Texas is different from both. All these geographic, demographic, historical, and ethnic differences did not prevent the formation of a common culture of home and family, a common image of woman, that stretched across the whole South in the 1830s and '40s. Southern women of the 1880s and the 1920s also shared behavior patterns whether they lived in Memphis or Mobile, in Richmond or Atlanta, or in smaller towns scattered across the South.

Life in the South broke apart between 1861 and 1865 and had to be put back together in a new mold. This fact is reflected in the materials upon which this book is based, and in the difference of tone and substance between Part I, which deals with the antebellum and war years, and Part II, which covers the time since 1865. I was able, for Part I, to rely on diaries and letters preserved in manuscript collections across the country. For the years after 1865 such materials are scarcer. Whether this reflects a cultural change, whether people became less inclined to keep diaries and write intense personal letters, whether such documents were not preserved or have not yet been deposited in manuscript collections, I do not know.

After 1865 something began which had rarely existed earlier. As they came out of the domestic circle to work, live, and act in a broader society, women began to create a public record. The materials for Part II are at once fuller and less revealing of individual personalities than those of Part I.

Writing this book has brought me into long arguments with male historians: is not my insistence upon paying so much attention to women simply a form of female chauvinism? To which I reply that my concern is less to do historical justice to women than to add to our understanding of what has been social reality.

Acknowledgments

As I survey the list of friends and colleagues who have made helpful suggestions about this book in manuscript I almost wonder who is left to read the published version. The dedication records the essential role Andrew Scott has played in the years of its gestation. Without his unswerving conviction that it could be done, it couldn't have. Oscar Handlin's ability to combine the twin incentives of praise for progress and scorn for sloth in the right proportions is remarkable. This undertaking owes him a great deal. Peter Filene of the University of North Carolina had the patience to read several drafts and the wit to abandon chivalry from the outset. Arthur Mann has improved nearly every page.

Some of the pleasantest experiences of my research grew out of interviews with six magnificent survivors of the great days of the woman movement, all in their eighties when I met them. Adele Clark was a Virginia suffragist and a leader of the League of Women Voters there. Kate Burr Johnson was the first woman Commissioner of Welfare in North Carolina. Gertrude Weil worked for suffrage in North Carolina and continued to be an active social reformer for the following half-century. Jessie Daniel Ames was a suffragist in Texas, an organizer of the League of Women Voters, and the prime mover of the Association of Southern Women for the Prevention of Lynching. Mary O. Cowper, secretary of the North Carolina League of Women Voters in the 1920s, continued the rest of her life as an active reformer, especially in the cause of child welfare. Jeannette Rankin, a Montana suffragist, was the first woman elected to the Congress of the United States; she now lives in Watkinsville, Georgia, and at last report was leading the anti-Vietnam movement in her locality.

For help of various kinds I am grateful to Daniel Aaron, Annette Baxter, Barbara Cleaveland, Carl Degler, Robert Durden, Lucy Somerville Howorth, Edward James, Joseph Katz, Jane de Hart and Donald Mathews, Sidney and Elizabeth Nathans, Orest Ranum, Willie Lee Rose, Harriet Simons, Allen Spalt, Julia Cherry Spruill, Edgar Thompson, George Tindall, Richard Watson, Frederick Wyatt, and Louise M. Young. David and Rebecca Scott listened to drafts of chapters and offered trenchant comments across the generation divide.

Librarians and archivists are the historian's secret weapon. I am especially grateful to James Patton, Isaac Copeland, Carolyn A. Wallace, and Anna Brooke Allan of the Southern Historical Collection at the University of North Carolina; to Mattie Russell and Virginia Gray of the Manuscripts Department of the William R. Perkins Library at Duke; and to Barbara M. Solomon and Janet James, successive directors of the Schlesinger Library at Radcliffe. I am also indebted to staff members of the Division of Manuscripts at the Library of Congress, the Manuscript Division of the Howard Tilton Memorial Library at Tulane, the Department of Archives and Manuscripts at Louisiana State University, the Frances Willard Memorial Library at Evanston, and the Division of Manuscripts at the University of Georgia. Florence Blakely, Mary Canada, and Pattie McIntyre, reference librarians at Duke and the University of North Carolina, have solved many problems for me. With all this help, the inadequacies are no one's fault but my own.

A great part of the writing of the book was made possible by a grant from the National Endowment for the Humanities, and in addition I have had indispensable support over the years from the Research Council of Duke University.

I must also record the contribution of Marie Alston Lee whose capacity to practice the traditional virtues of the southern lady has given me the opportunity to practice the freedoms of the new woman.

Some of the material in Part II appeared in a different form in two articles—"The 'New Woman' in the New South," *South Atlantic Quarterly* 65 (Autumn 1962): 471–83, and "After Suffrage: Southern Women in the Twenties," *Journal of Southern History* 30 (August 1964): 298–318—and is used here with the permission of those journals.

Part one
THE ANTE-BELLUM LADY

. . . a Southern matron is ever
idolized and almost worshipped by
her dependents, and beloved by
her children, to whom no word
ever sounds half so sweet as
mother and for whom no place
possesses one half the charms of
home.

Daniel R. Hundley,
Social Relations in Our Southern States

1

The Image: Queen of the Home

If talking could make it so, antebellum southern women of the upper class would have been the most perfect examples of womankind yet seen on earth. If praise could satisfy all of woman's needs, they would also have been the happiest. Literary journals, sermons, novels, commencement addresses—wherever men spoke there was praise of Woman, and exhortation to further perfection.

This marvelous creation was described as a submissive wife whose reason for being was to love, honor, obey, and occasionally amuse her husband, to bring up his children and manage his household. Physically weak, and "formed for the less laborious occupations," she depended upon male protection. To secure this protection she was endowed with the capacity to "create a magic spell" over any man in her vicinity. She was timid and modest, beautiful and graceful, "the most fascinating being in creation . . . the delight and charm of every circle she moves in."

Part of her charm lay in her innocence. The less a woman knew of life, Ellen Glasgow once remarked bitterly, the better she was supposed to be able to deal with it. Her mind was not logical, but in the absence of reasoning capacity her sensibility and intuition were highly developed. It was, indeed, to her advantage that "the play of instincts and of the feelings is not cramped by the controlling influence of logic and reason." She was capable of acute perceptions about human relationships, and was a creature of tact, discernment, sympathy, and compassion. It was her nature to be self-denying, and she was given to suffering in silence, a characteristic said to endear her to men. Less endearing, perhaps, but no less natural, was her piety and her tendency to "restrain man's natural vice and immorality." She was thought to be "most deeply interested in the success of every scheme which curbs the passions and enforces a true morality." She was a natural teacher, and a wise counselor to her husband and children.[1]

Thomas Nelson Page, writing many years after the Civil War, summed up the image:

Her life was one long act of devotion,—devotion to God, devotion to her husband, devotion to her children, devotion to her servants, to the poor, to humanity. Nothing happened within the range of her knowledge that her sympathy did not reach and her charity and wisdom did not ameliorate. She was the head and font of the church. . . . The training of her children was her work. She watched over them, inspired them, led them, governed them; her will impelled them; her word to them, as to her servants, was law. She reaped the reward . . . their sympathy and tenderness were hers always, and they worshipped her.[2]

Even a realist like Augustus Baldwin Longstreet was obviously influenced by the image when he came to describe a southern matron in one of his stories:

. . . pious but not austere, cheerful, but not light; generous but not prodigal; economical, but not close; hospitable but not extravagant. . . . To have heard her converse you would have supposed she did nothing but read, to have looked through the departments of her household you would have supposed she never read. . . . Everything under her care went on with perfect system.[3]

1. The quotations and descriptions here are from the *Southern Literary Messenger* 1, (1835), but similar ones are found in the *Southern Ladies Companion,* the *Southern Quarterly Review,* and many speeches, novels, memoirs, and poems.
2. *Social Life in Old Virginia* (New York: Charles Scribner's Sons, 1897), pp. 38–42.
3. *Georgia Scenes,* new ed. (New York: Harper & Bros., 1897), pp. 108–9.

Oddly enough this paragon of virtue was thought to need the direction and control of some man. A person identified only as "president of the oldest college in Virginia" published a letter to his newly married daughter in an early issue of the *Southern Literary Messenger*. The wife's conduct alone, he asserted, determined the happiness or misery of a marriage. She must resolve at the outset never to oppose her husband, never to show displeasure, no matter what he might do. A man had a right to expect his wife to place perfect confidence in his judgment and to believe that he always knew best. "A difference with your husband ought to be considered the greatest calamity," wrote the father, adding that a woman who permitted differences to occur could expect to lose her husband's love and all hope of happiness. He concluded with the usual injunctions that she should be amiable, sweet, prudent, and devoted, that she should regulate her servants with a kind but firm hand, cultivate her mind by reading history and not corrupt it with novels, and manage her domestic concerns with neatness, order, economy, and judgment.[4]

A novelist echoed the opinions of the college president. "In the heart of woman, uncorrupted by a false philosophy which would unfit her for her proper sphere, the proudest feeling is that of admiration for her husband. . . . this is as God meant it should be. To this state the natural feelings of a woman's heart will tend, let quacks in education do what they will."[5]

4. *Southern Literary Messenger* 1 (1835): 187–88. This was probably Adam P. Empie, D.D., who was president of William and Mary College, 1827–35. See *Catalogue of the College of William and Mary from Its Foundation to the Present Time* (Williamsburg, 1869).

5. Beverly Tucker, *George Balcombe* (New York: Harper & Bros., 1836), 1: 274.

From earliest childhood girls were trained to the ideals of perfection and submission. A magazine for children published in Charleston, recording the death of a seven-year-old, spoke of her as "peculiarly amiable and engaging; her behaviour marked with a delicate sense of propriety, happily mingled with an artless innocence." She was praised for being kind and considerate to her servants. The fiction in the same magazine was filled with pious, obedient little girls.[6] Boarding schools for young ladies, to which more and more girls were sent as the century wore on, emphasized correct female behavior more than intellectual development. In at least one school the girls wrote their English compositions on such subjects as modesty, benevolence, and the evils of reading novels.[7]

By the time they arrived at their teens most girls had absorbed the injunctions of the myth. One young woman wrote in her diary that she longed to die because she had not found a husband, adding, "I know I would make a faithful, obedient wife, loving with all my heart, yielding entire trust in my husband."[8]

The image of the submissive woman was reinforced by evangelical theology. Daniel R. Hundley, a young Alabama lawyer who wrote a sociological analysis of the antebellum South, relied on Saint Paul's authority for asserting that women should "content themselves with their humble house-

6. *The Rosebud* 1, no. 13 (24 November, 1831): 521 and passim.
7. "A Folder of Student Compositions," 1840, Iverson L. Brooks Papers, Southern Historical Collection, University of North Carolina (hereafter cited as SHC UNC).
8. "Anonymous Diary of a Young Woman Living near Natchez," Manuscript Department, William R. Perkins Library, Duke University (hereafter cited as MS Dept., Duke).

hold duties." [9] Southern pulpits repeated the apostle's injunction that women should keep silent in the churches. One minister argued that women needed "the hope and prospects of religion more . . . than the other sex" to soften the pains of living and help women bear with patience and submission the inevitable trials of life, among which he suggested might be "a husband of acid temper." [10] A North Carolina doctor wrote that "God in his inscrutable wisdom has appointed a place and duty for females *out of which* they can neither accomplish their destiny nor secure their happiness ! !" [11]

Southern women sought diligently to live up to the prescriptions, to attain the perfection and the submissiveness demanded of them by God and man. John Donald Wade, whose researches into the life of Augustus Baldwin Longstreet reinforced his understanding of the social history of middle Georgia, concluded that "men found intelligence in woman a quality that in general distressed more than it pleased. When they did not openly condemn they treated it with insulting condescension. *The women proved themselves marvelously adaptable.*" [12] A woman novelist suggested something about the ongoing struggle to live up to the expectations of men:

> To repress a harsh answer, to confess a fault, and to stop (right or wrong) in the midst of self-defence, in gentle submission, sometimes requires a struggle like life and death; but

9. *Social Relations in Our Southern States* (New York: H. B. Price, 1860), p. 74.

10. D. A. Clark, "Beauties of Female Piety," quoted in Guion G. Johnson *Ante-Bellum North Carolina* (Chapel Hill; University of North Carolina Press, 1937), pp. 228–29.

11. Dr. James A. Norcum to Mary B. Harvey 25 May 1848, Norcum Papers, N.C. Department of Archives and History, Raleigh.

12. *Augustus Baldwin Longstreet* (New York: Macmillan, 1924), p. 67. Italics added.

these *three* efforts are the golden threads with which domestic happiness is woven; once begin the fabric with this woof, and trials shall not break or sorrow tarnish it.

Men are not often unreasonable; their difficulties lie in not understanding the moral and physical structure of our sex. . . . How clear it is, then, that woman loses by petulance and recrimination! Her first study must be self-control, almost to hypocrisy. A good wife must smile amid a thousand perplexities, and clear her voice to tones of cheerfulness when her frame is drooping with disease or else languish alone.[13]

Women made heroic efforts to live up to what was expected of them. One, who could hardly bear the sound of her husband tuning his violin, bit her lip and said nothing, murmuring about self-abnegation.[14] There was no rest for the conscience. "We owe it to our husbands, children and friends," wrote a Louisiana housewife, "to represent as nearly as possible the ideal which they hold so dear." [15] " 'Tis man's to act, 'tis woman's to endure," reflected an Alabama novelist in the midst of trials with a husband she did not much respect, and financial problems beyond her power to solve.[16] Women were made, indeed, the long-suffering wife of the violinist concluded, "to suffer and be strong." [17] "Give me a double portion of the grace of thy Spirit that I may learn meekness," wrote the self-flagellating wife of a minister.[18]

13. Caroline Gilman, *Recollections of a Southern Matron* (New York: Harper & Bros., 1839), p. 256.

14. Ella Gertrude Clanton Thomas Diary, 30 November 1858, MS Dept., Duke.

15. Caroline Merrick to "my dear friend," 23 May 1857, Department of Archives and Manuscripts, Louisiana State University, Baton Rouge (hereafter cited as Dept. of Archives, LSU).

16. Caroline Lee Hentz Diary, 5 March 1836, SHC UNC.

17. E. G. C. Thomas Diary, New Year's Day 1858, MS Dept., Duke.

18. Lucilla McCorkle Diary, 12 July 1846, SHC UNC.

Even more effort, if possible, went into the struggle to live up to what God was presumed to expect of women. A young bride laid down a program for herself:

1. To read the Bible and pray after rising in the morning and sometime after breakfast.
2. To pray again before dinner and read the Bible in the evening and pray before bed.
3. To obey my husband in all things reasonable.
4. "I will endeavor to use patience and forebearance towards my son [her husband's son by an earlier marriage] and correct him in a spirit of mildness for every offense of which he may be guilty.
5. "I will endeavor to offend not with the tongue, but hold it in with bit and bridle and speak charitably of all persons."
6. "I will endeavor to do good unto all as far as it is in my power, especially unto the household of faith."
7. "I will endeavor to subdue every evil propensity by the assistance of Divine Grace, and by practicing that degree of fasting and abstinence which my health will admit of." [19]

This same woman kept a religious diary devoted entirely to daily meditations and painful examination of her progress in the endless struggle for religious perfection. Shortly after her marriage she begged God to cleanse her of secret faults, to save her from impatience and hastiness of temper, and to give her "perfect resignation to Thy Holy Will concerning me." In succeeding entries she deplored her own hardness of heart and expressed guilt when she did not bear severe pain with Christian fortitude.

This was not just one aberrant perfectionist. There are numerous similar letters and diaries. "I feel this day heavy and sad and I would ask myself why and the answer is I

19. Diary of Anne Beale Davis, Beale-Davis Papers, SHC UNC.

feel cold in religious matters oh why am I thus?"[20] "I feel that I am worthless and through the merits of Christ's all-atoning blood alone can I be saved."[21] "Mr B. [her husband] says we must try to live holier. Oh that I could. Spent some time today reading, weeping and praying."[22] "Help me O Lord for I am poor and weak, help me for I am desolate, in Thee alone have I hope."[23] As for myself I find my heart so full of sinful feelings that I am ready to say 'I am chief of sinners.'"[24] "Lord I feel that my heart is a cage of unclean beasts."[25] "I see so much of sin, so many things to correct, that I almost despair of being a perfect christian."[26] "Oh! for an increased degree of peace to know and do my redeemers will, to live more as I should."[27]

The biblical verse most frequently quoted in southern women's diaries was from Jeremiah: "The heart is deceitful above all things and desperately wicked: who can know it?"[28] There are references to sins too awful even to be recorded in a private journal, accompanied by allusions to cold hearts.

Many women assumed that if they were unhappy or discontented in the "sphere to which God had appointed them" it must be their own fault and that by renewed effort

20. Diary of Myra Smith, 17 April 1851, Somerville-Howorth Papers, Schlesinger Library, Radcliffe College.
21. Ibid., January 1852.
22. Diary of Fannie Moore Webb Bumpas, 5 March 1842, SHC UNC.
23. Diary of Charlotte Beatty, 1843, SHC UNC.
24. Sarah Wadley Journal, 4 February 1863, SHC UNC. She was eighteen at the time!
25. Lucilla McCorkle Diary, May 1846, SHC UNC.
26. Annie to Lollie, 14 December 1859, in Lucy Cole Burwell Papers, MS Dept., Duke.
27. E. G. C. Thomas Diary, 8 April 1855, MS Dept., Duke.
28. Jere. 17:9.

they could do better. "My besetting sins are a roving mind and an impetuous spirit," wrote one woman whose diary is filled with admonitions to herself to be systematic, diligent, prudent, economical, and patient with her servants.[29] Josephine Clay Habersham was a gentle and gifted woman who presided with skill and dignity over a large plantation in eastern Georgia. A devoted mother who could write, "I wish always to have a sweet babe to mind, care for and love," she still felt it necessary to make a constant effort to cultivate a cheerful spirit, to ask God for help with her "dull and wayward heart," and to ask forgiveness for not being a more faithful servant.[30] A girl of eighteen prayed to be useful and bemoaned the "vain desires that every now and then trouble this prevailing one [to love God] and my flesh is so weak, I am always failing." [31]

Women whose families and friends thought them "spotless" were themselves convinced that their souls were in danger. One prayed to God to be delivered from the "serpent whose folds are around my limbs; his sting in my heart." [32] A Mississippi woman found her mind "sunk in a state of apathy from which I can with difficulty arouse myself" and was sure that this was because she had neglected her duty and transgressed God's holy laws. She was constantly concerned lest "the world and its cares have too large a share of my time and affections." [33]

29. Lucilla McCorkle Diary, 1 December 1850, SHC UNC.

30. *Ebb Tide,* ed. Spencer B. King (Athens, Ga: University of Georgia Press, 1958), pp. 77, 103–4.

31. Sarah Wadley Journal, 20 August 1863, SHC UNC.

32. Diary of Mrs. Isaac Hilliard, 21 April 1850, Dept. of Archives, LSU.

33. Diary of Myra Smith, 15 December 1850, Schlesinger Library, Radcliffe.

For many of these women the brief span of earthly life was chiefly important as preparation for eternity, and much of their self-exhortation centered on being ready to die. They prayed for the will to "overcome every evil propensity . . . to be calm and collected at all times," so as to be ready to depart from the world at a moment's notice in a state of grace, or for the power to bring other sinners to the "throne of peace." [34] Such women were cast into deep depression when they gave way to temper, slapped a child, or admonished a slave. One woman scolded herself, "I am not as much engaged in religion as I should be . . . too worldly." [35] An unattainable perfection was the only standard.

There is little doubt that religious faith served an important function at a time when many children and adults died for no apparent reason. A firm belief that death was a manifestation of God's will made it easier to bear what otherwise would have been an intolerable burden. It is also clear that the requirements for salvation dovetailed neatly with the secular image of women. Religious women were persuaded that the very qualities which made any human being a rich, interesting, assertive personality—a roving mind, spirit, ambition—were propensities to be curbed. No matter what secret thoughts a woman might have about her own abilities, religion confirmed what society told her— namely, that she was inferior to men.

The language of piety and the desire for salvation, the belief in an eternal life, were not, of course, confined to women. The same phrases abound in the letters, diaries, and sermons of many men. The significant difference was that

34. Diary of Anne Beale Davis, 14 August 1842, SHC UNC; E. G. C. Thomas Diary, 8 April 1855, MS Dept., Duke.
35. Diary of Fannie Moore Webb Bumpas, 26 June 1842, SHC UNC.

for men submission to God's will in spiritual matters was considered to be perfectly compatible with aggressive behavior and a commanding position in life. Men expected to be obeyed by women, children, and slaves, to be the decision makers and the ultimate source of secular authority.

Daniel Hundley's myth of the southern gentleman complements the image of the southern lady. The gentleman, Hundley insisted, in addition to being finely formed and highly educated, was firm, commanding, and a perfect patriarch. "The natural dignity of manner peculiar to the southern gentleman is doubtless owing to his habitual use of authority from his earliest years." The weakness and dependence of women was thrown into bold relief by his virility and mastery of his environment.[36] Husbands were frequently referred to in the words used for God: Lord and Master.

The rigid definition of the proper role and behavior of southern women requires explanation. It is not that the constellation of ideas which constituted the image of the southern lady was peculiar to the American South; men in Victorian England conjured up a similar myth in poems like Coventry Patmore's "The Angel in the House."[37] Harriet Martineau was speaking of all American women, not just those of the South, when she described them as lying down at night "full of self-reproach for the want of piety which they do not know how to attain."[38] But, as William R. Taylor has noted, southern plantation novelists were "fanat-

36. *Social Relations,* pp. 56–61.
37. Walter Houghton, *The Victorian Frame of Mind* (New Haven: Yale University Press, 1957), pp. 341–430.
38. *Society in America,* abridged version (New York: Doubleday, Anchor, 1962), p. 337.

ical" in idolizing and idealizing southern women. The evidence adduced in this chapter bears out his observation with respect to southern men in general.[39]

Such men continued an old tradition in Western history. The myth of the lady was associated with medieval chivalry. Books of advice on proper behavior for both men and women dated back to the invention of printing. Castiglione's *The Courtier,* a sixteenth-century book of etiquette, set the style for such books, and by the eighteenth century books specifically directed to women were widely read in England and in America. Usually written by men, they emphasized the softness, purity, and spirituality of women while denying them intellectual capacity. Women were instructed to please their husbands, attend to their physical needs, cover up their indiscretions, and give them no cause for worry. All such descriptions and injunctions were included in the southern creed.[40]

But the fact that such ideas had been around for a long time does not explain why they were so enthusiastically embraced by antebellum southerners. Other models were available for a sparsely settled rural society. The good

39. *Cavalier and Yankee* (New York: Braziller, 1963), pp. 123–55.

40. See Chilton Latham Powell, *English Domestic Relations, 1487–1653* (New York: Columbia University Press, 1917), for a description of early English advice books. Janet Wilson James, "Changing Ideas about Women in the United States, 1776–1825," 1954 Ph.D. dissertation in the Schlesinger Library, Radcliffe College, is an excellent study of the advice books which were widely read in America. A collection of these books may also be found in the Schlesinger Library. Eileen Power, *Medieval People* (London: Methuen, 1924), chapter 4, provides a charming exposition of one such book, which, on the wife's duty to the husband, offered a direct forecast of the southern image: "She is to be loving, humble, obedient, careful and thoughtful for his person, silent regarding his secrets, and patient if he is foolish and allows his heart to stray toward other women."

woman of Proverbs, for example, who worked willingly with her hands, got up early and set all in her household to work, bought and sold land, and didn't worry about her appearance might have been an excellent ideal.[41] Why was she not chosen?

We know very little about the relationship of ideology to social structures and understand very little about the social consequences of unconscious needs. Even so, it is possible to speculate that, as with so much else in the antebellum South, slavery had a good deal to do with the ideal of the southern lady. Because they owned slaves and thus maintained a traditional landowning aristocracy, southerners tenaciously held on to the patriarchal family structure. The patriarchy had been the norm in seventeenth-century England. Transported to Virginia and adopted as a social pattern by the planters there, it lived on into the nineteenth century in the whole South.[42] A future officer of the Confederacy explained the theory of the family common among his contemporaries, and related it directly to the institution of slavery:

The Slave Institution of the South increases the tendency to dignify the family. Each planter is in fact a Patriarch—his position compels him to be a ruler in his household. From early youth, his children and servants look up to him as the head,

41. Prov. 31.
42. William Byrd to Charles, Earl of Orkney, 5 July 1726, describing his life as a patriarch, in the *Virginia Magazine of History and Biography* 32 (January 1924): 27. See also Peter Laslett, introduction to Robert Filmer, *Patriarchal:* "It is worth pointing out . . . that the descendants of the Virginia planters, who became the slaveholders of the Southern States, were the heads of a classic type of patriarchal household, so that it survived until the middle of the nineteenth century even in so rationalistic and equalitarian a society as the U.S.A." (Oxford: B. Blackwell, 1949), p. 26.

and obedience and subordination become important elements of education. . . . Domestic relations become those which are most prized.[43]

Women, along with children and slaves, were expected to recognize their proper and subordinate place and to be obedient to the head of the family. Any tendency on the part of any of the members of the system to assert themselves against the master threatened the whole, and therefore slavery itself. It was no accident that the most articulate spokesman for slavery were also eloquent exponents of the subordinate role of women. George Fitzhugh, perhaps the most noted and certainly among the most able of these spokesmen, wrote, for example:

So long as she is nervous, fickle, capricious, delicate, diffident and dependent, man will worship and adore her. Her weakness is her strength, and her true art is to cultivate and improve that weakness. Woman naturally shrinks from public gaze, and from the struggle and competition of life. . . . in truth, woman, like children, has but one right and that is the right to protection. The right to protection involves the obligation to obey. A husband, a lord and master, whom she should love, honor and obey, nature designed for every woman. . . . If she be obedient she stands little danger of maltreatment.[44]

If the need to maintain the slave system contributed to the insistence upon perfect, though submissive, women, so did the simple fact that a male-dominated society was good for men. Some of the characteristics demanded of the southern lady were also expected of women in other parts of the

43. Christopher C. G. Memminger, Lecture before the Young Men's Library Association of Augusta, Georgia, 1851, quoted in W. S. Jenkins, *Pro-Slavery Thought in the Old South* (Chapel Hill: University of North Carolina Press, 1935), p. 210.

44. *Sociology for the South* (Richmond: Morris, 1854), pp. 214–15.

United States and require no more complex explanation than that any ruling group can find a theory to justify its position. Like aristocrats, Communists, and bourgeois businessmen, southern men had no trouble finding theoretical support for a way of life that was decidedly to their advantage. Obedient, faithful, submissive women strengthened the image of men who thought themselves vigorous, intelligent, commanding leaders.

Such women also contributed considerably to manly creature comforts. Ellen Glasgow put it this way in one of her novels:

The cares she met with such serenity had been too heavy for her strength; they had driven the bloom from her cheeks and the lustre from her eyes; and, though she had not faltered at her task, she had drooped daily and grown older than her years. The master might live with lavish disregard of the morrow, not the master's wife. For him were the open house, the shining table, the well-stocked wine cellar and the morning rides over the dewey fields; for her the care of her home and children, and of the souls and bodies of the black people that had been given into her hands.[45]

Despite the vigor of their statements, there is some evidence that southern men did not feel altogether secure in their self-proclaimed position of lord and master of the whole patriarchy. Fear lay beneath the surface of the flowery praise of woman and the insistence that God had made her the way men wanted her to be. Otherwise it is hard to see why men spent so much time and energy stating their position. One of Beverly Tucker's leading characters discussed the way he proposed to educate his daughter. She

45. *The Battle Ground* (New York: Doubleday & Page, 1902), p. 48.

must be raised, he said, to take for granted her husband's superiority, to rely on his wisdom, to take pride in his distinction. "Even should her faculties be superior to his, he cannot raise her so high but that she will still feel herself a creature of his hands." [46]

What were they afraid of, these would-be patriarchs who threatened to withdraw their love from women who disagreed with them or aspired to any forbidden activity? Partly, perhaps, that the women to whom they had granted the custody of conscience and morality might apply that conscience to male behavior—to sharp trading in the market place, to inordinate addiction to alcohol, to nocturnal visits to the slave quarters. Men were aware, too, that the woman who had been so firmly put in her place, the home, often showed unusual power within that restricted domain. She raised the children; she set the standards for behavior. In 1802 a visiting Englishman commented that in North Carolina "the legislative and executive powers of the house belong to the mistress, the master has nothing to do with administration; he is a monument of uxoriousness and passive endurance." [47] Two decades later a North Carolinian wrote to a friend contemplating matrimony that he must be "prepared to have his nose occasionally ground . . . and that he must not drink or play cards." [48] If women could exert so much power even in their restricted position who could tell what they might do with more freedom?

The omens were there to see. Southern men often identified the work of the hated abolitionists with the work of

46. *George Balcombe* (New York, 1836), 2:52.
47. John Davis, *Personal Adventures and Travels of Four and a Half Years in the United States of America,* quoted in Katherine Jones, *Plantation South* (Indianapolis: Bobbs-Merrill, 1957), p. 85.
48. Quoted in Johnson, *Ante-Bellum North Carolina,* p. 243.

"strong-minded" northern women. A Virginian wrote to a friend in 1853:

You have doubtless seen in the newspapers the struggle we had with the strong-minded women as they call themselves in the World Temperance Convention. If you have seen a true account of the matter you will see that we gained a perfect triumph, and I believe have given a rebuke to this most impudent clique of unsexed females and rampant abolitionists which must put down the petticoats—at least as far as their claim to take the platforms of public debate and enter into all the rough and tumble of the war of words.

His college professor correspondent replied: "I most heartily rejoice with you in the defeat of those shameless amazons." [49] It was a paradox that men who asserted that God made woman as they wished her to be, or that the feminine qualities they admired were given by nature, were afraid that women would break out of the God-given and natural mode of behavior.

If these speculations ring true, one pressing question still remains. Since the ideal of perfection placed a great strain upon women, why did they tolerate their role? One reason is suggested by the early indoctrination already mentioned: the institutions and mores of the society all pointed in the same direction. Churches, schools, parents, books, magazines, all promulgated the same message: be a lady and you will be loved and respected and supported. If you defy the

49. John Hartwell Cocke is the writer of the first letter. He is discussed in Clement Eaton's *The Mind of the Old South* (Baton Rouge: Louisiana State University Press, 1964) as "the liberal mind in a southern context" (pp. 11–12). Obviously his liberalism did not extend to women who chose to be "strong-minded!" George Fitzhugh was the recipient of the letter.

pattern and behave in ways considered unladylike you will be unsexed, rejected, unloved, and you will probably starve.

The persistence of the complementary images of the soft, submissive, perfect woman and of the strong, commanding, intelligent, and dominant man in the face of an exigent reality that often called for quite different qualities suggests that these images had deep significance for the men and women who believed in them. A society increasingly threatened from the outside had every reason to try to diminish internal threats to its stability. George Fitzhugh made this quite explicit when he equated any change in the role of women *or* in the institution of slavery with the downfall of the family and the consequent demise of society. If the distance between the myth and reality became so great that it could not be overlooked, then the situation might be threatening indeed.

Though many southern women were worried about slavery, few had any vision of a society different from the one they knew. Perhaps they, too, sensed a threat of social disorganization inherent in any challenge to male dominance. For whatever reasons, most of them tried to live up to the Sisyphean task expected of them.

... when a young man is
about to get him a wife, the first
inquiry he makes is, Has such a
young lady much prop-
erty ... ?

Raleigh Register, 12 October 1808

The gentle and refined lady
who was mistress of a Virginia
plantation would have stood
poorly among her peers, would
have failed in the eyes of her
husband and children, and fallen
below the ideal she set for
herself, if she had not been
familiar with a score of trades.

Orra Langhorne,
Southern Sketches from Virginia

2

The Reality:
Love, Marriage,
Work, and
Family Life

The mythology assured every young woman that she was a belle, endowed with magic powers to attract men and bend them to her will. This was comforting, since she was also assured that God had created her to be a wife and mother, and men did the proposing. Parents, boarding schools, advice books, and friends tried to help her make up for any natural deficiencies by emphasizing the power of manner, charm, "accomplishments," and virtue. And since God had created women to be wives and mothers it was logical that he had also, as George Fitzhugh cheerfully asserted, designed a lord and master for every woman.

In spite of the combined efforts of nature and nurture, however, girls might well be discouraged by their real life experience. To be sure, in areas where there were enough men to go around, most women did marry, and marry young, but romantic expectations and the myth of the southern gentleman might hinder rather than help in reaching that all-important goal. One young woman put the matter bluntly in her diary:

Shall I say here if not aloud why I have never yet fallen in love? Simply because I have yet to meet the man I would be willing to acknowledge as my lord and master. For unconfessed to myself, and until very recently, I have dressed up an image in my heart and have unconsciously worshipped it under the name of Beau Ideal. . . . my lord and master must be some one I shall never have to blush for, or be ashamed to acknowledge, the one that after God I shall most venerate and respect. . . . He must be as brave as a man can be.[1]

If the neighborhood failed to yield a Beau Ideal, or if the magic spell turned out to be inadequate to attract him, romantic images of love gave way to more pragmatic consid-

1. Sarah Morgan Diary, 6 May 1862, MS Dept., Duke.

erations. Proximity, a thoughtful consideration of land and family connections, or the painful fear of being an old maid were often the basis for marriage. A South Carolina matron demonstrated a mother's view of these matters when she noted in her diary that all the world seemed to be getting married except her own children. "I wish a suitable offer would come Elizabeth's way . . . and that Berkeley would find some nice girl with a little money to get married to."[2] And when her brother married she observed with pleasure that his wife was of good family, would have $40,000 in peacetime, and "is a sensible woman, quite accustomed to society, and will manage Charles and take care of his money & make him very happy."[3]

Also in the privacy of a diary, a wealthy North Carolina matron reflected upon the order of concerns her recently widowed sister might feel. Her brother-in-law had been good company, but more important, the "position and political importance she derived from him and in which she took such pride" would make the bereavement severe.[4]

A great lady in Charleston, a sophisticated observer of society wherever she went, took a cynical view of all talk of romantic love.

It is an odd thing. In all my life how many persons have I seen in love? Not a half-dozen, and yet I am a tolerably close observer, a faithful watcher of men and manners. Society has been for me only an enlarged field for character study. Flirtation is the business of society. That is play at love making; it

2. Diary of Meta Morris Grimball, 10 December 1860, SHC UNC.
3. Ibid., 19 October 1862.
4. Catherine Edmonston, "Diary of Looking Glass Plantation," ed. James Patton and Beth Crabtree; typescript in Dr. Patton's possession. Original 4-vol. manuscript in N.C. Dept. of Archives and History, Raleigh.

begins in vanity, it ends in vanity. It is spurred on by idleness and a want of other excitement. . . . it is a pleasant but very foolish game.[5]

⌁ In private letters and diaries, as opposed to fiction and poetry, pragmatic considerations loomed larger than romance. A Methodist minister in North Carolina decided after the death of his parents that he should find a wife, lest he lose touch with humanity. He looked over the available girls, chose one, and after a few months noted in his diary that there was no disadvantage to a minister in having a wife as long as she was the right kind.[6] A young student at the University of North Carolina recorded his intention to call upon a young lady whom he had never met with an eye to courting her, apparently because he had heard she was both beautiful and rich. After one visit he unsuccessfully begged leave to "address" her. Rejected, he turned his attention to another lady, whom he regretfully gave up when he discovered she had no dowry.[7] William Dorsey Pender, a gentleman of a slightly later generation, upbraided by his wife about an old flame, replied quickly, "I never loved her, *nor did my judgement sanction any connection with the family.*"[8]

In middle Georgia, an area inhabited by solid up-country planters, girls began very early to accumulate a hope chest. Marriages at fourteen or fifteen were common. The girl who

5. Mary Boykin Chesnut, *A Diary from Dixie* (Boston: Houghton Mifflin, Sentry edition, 1951), p. 463.

6. Diary of Sidney Bumpas, SHC UNC.

7. John L. Sanders, ed., "Diary of Ruffin Wirt Tomlinson," *North Carolina Historical Review* 30 (January–April 1953).

8. William W. Hassler, ed., *The General to His Lady: The Civil War Letters of William Dorsey Pender to Fanny Pender* (Chapel Hill: University of North Carolina Press, 1966), p. 206. Italics added.

had many beaux was envied, and families with a "houseful
of old maids" pitied. "If there was a prospect of plantation
or slaves as a dowry there was a rush into matrimony,"
though such hasty decisions might lead later to regret.[9]
Much of the courting was done on horseback as young
people went to and from church. When land was plentiful,
so that each child could have a farm, parents encouraged
early marriage.[10]

For all the insistence that family life and motherhood
were the central meaning of woman's life, marriages were
often contracted casually. A Virginia Methodist minister
took his audience to task for the haste with which both men
and women rushed into matrimony only to discover when it
was too late that they were "married but not mated. A
marries for a freak just to be talked about; B for spite; C,
to be revenged on an enemy . . . G to avoid being teased on
the subject by gossips . . . and others they know not
why." [11]

If pragmatism or impulse or necessity for the most part
outweighed romance in the marriage market, there were
enough real life love affairs to keep the myth alive. Joseph
Jones, scion of an influential Georgia family who had been
north for his medical education, was appointed to the faculty of the Georgia Medical College in Augusta. There he
met the daughter of a local minister with whom he was soon
corresponding daily. The order of virtues Jones listed in a
letter to his parents is interesting: "The intelligence, charity

9. Rebecca Latimer Felton, *Country Life in Georgia in the Days of
My Youth* (Atlanta: Index Printing Co. 1919), pp. 62–63.
10. Judge Garnett Andrews, *Reminiscences of an Old Georgia Lawyer*
(Atlanta: Franklin Steam Printing House, 1870), passim.
11. John C. Bayley, *Marriage As It Is and Should Be* (New York:
M. W. Dodd, 1857), pp. 43–44.

and piety of Miss Caroline S. Davis have completely won my heart." Both Jones and his fiancée were inclined to literary expression, he resorting to Aristotle for help in making his points and she making generous use of Elizabeth Barrett Browning. They were married, and when he went into the army in 1861 the correspondence was resumed. In it they left a record of a devoted marriage, which lasted until Mrs. Jones's early death.[12]

If the actual process of finding a mate did not always follow the romantic prescription, so, too, the everyday realities of married women's lives were different from anything the image would lead one to expect. The shock of sudden transition from the life of a carefree, sought-after girl to one circumscribed by matronly responsibilities was recorded over and over. "She often told us of her distress on realising for the first time the responsibilities devolving upon the mistress of a large plantation, and the nights of sorrow and tears these thoughts had given her," a Virginia woman wrote of her mother.[13] It was two years before Thomas Dabney's shy sixteen-year old bride could summon the courage to take charge of her servants, and not all men were as patient as Dabney, who at the time of his marriage was a twenty-seven-year-old widower.[14] The wife of a South Carolina planter, similarly dismayed to find what was expected

12. Joseph Jones to C. C. Jones, 17 February 1859, C. C. Jones Papers, Manuscripts Division, Howard Tilton Memorial Library, Tulane University. Both sides of the Jones-Davis correspondence have been preserved. Some of the letters are in the C. C. Jones Papers at Tulane and others in the Joseph Jones Papers at LSU.

13. Letitia Burwell, *A Girl's Life in Virginia before the War* (New York: Frederick A. Stokes, 1895), p. 23.

14. Susan Dabney Smedes, *Memorials of a Southern Planter,* ed. Fletcher Green (New York: Knopf, 1965), p. 19.

of her, went to her husband in tears saying she had no idea what to do with so many servants. In this case the husband simply pointed out that she had to begin somewhere, and that once begun she would find plenty to do. "And truly she found it so," wrote her daughter. "But it took all her own precious time to direct and plan and carry out the work. The calls to do something which seemed important and necessary were incessant."[15] "I was so young a bride, only seventeen . . . that I felt no dread whatever of my new duties as a mistress . . . and felt rather nonplussed when brought into contact with reality," wrote a North Carolina plantation mistress.[16] A South Carolina matron summed up the whole matter: "After the first year, no man can tell whether he married for love or for money."[17] Whatever had occasioned the match, the responsibilities of wives were much the same everywhere.

The precise meaning of "work" varied with station in society, economic condition, and geographic location, but women of leisure were hard to find. The ordinary planter's wife led a very demanding life, and the wife of the yeoman farmer differed from her more affluent sister chiefly in the amount of work she did with her own hands. Even the poor white woman, whose husband, according to legend, was largely employed in hunting, fishing, and whittling, worked much harder than her spouse, since someone had to keep the family alive. In *Plain Folk in the Old South,* Frank Owsley suggests that many of the people taken by casual travelers

15. Elizabeth Allston Pringle, *Chronicles of Chicora Wood* (New York: Charles Scribner's Sons, 1922), p. 61.

16. Margaret Devereux, *Plantation Sketches* (Cambridge, Mass.: Privately printed, 1946), p. 5.

17. Chesnut, *Diary from Dixie,* p. 177.

to be "poor whites" were really herdsmen who only appeared to be idle and shiftless, but he adds that their wives
did not give even the appearance of idleness, as they "hoed
the corn, cooked the dinner or plied the loom, or even came
out and took up the ax and cut the wood with which to cook
the dinner." [18]

There were a few urban great ladies whose slaves were so
well trained that their own duties were largely administrative. Some wives of congressmen "boarded" in Washington
and had time for a gay social existence. But such relatively
idle southern women were rare.[19]

A planter's wife was, as a Virginia lady noted, a good
housekeeper whether she wanted to be or not. To be so was
"a necessity thrust upon her by circumstances. . . . Her
large family, the immense retinue of slaves who all had to
be fed, clothed, nursed, not to mention the incessant and
heavy demands of hospitality, made her the real burden-
bearer of the community." [20] "From supervising the sitting
of turkeys to fighting a pestilence, there was nothing which
was not her work," added another Virginian.[21] "Mother
Williams works harder than any Northern farmer's wife I
know," wrote the surprised bride of a southern planter, who

18. Owsley, *Plain Folk in the Old South* (Baton Rouge: Louisiana
State University Press, 1949), p. 35.

19. Mary Boykin Chesnut is an excellent example of the first, and her
leisure was greater because she had no children. Virginia Clay-Clopton
described life in the congressional circle of which both she and Mrs.
Chesnut were a part in that decade. See *A Belle of the Fifties: Memoirs
of Mrs. Clay of Alabama, covering Social and Political Life in Washington and the South 1853–66. Put into narrative form by Ada Sterling*
(New York: William Heinemann, 1905).

20. Sally McCarty Pleasants, *Old Virginia Ways and Days* (Menasha,
Wis., 1916), p. 34.

21. Thomas Nelson Page, *Social Life in Old Virginia* (New York:
Charles Scribner's Sons, 1897), p. 38.

had pictured herself marrying into a life of ease.[22] "This is the first leisure moment I have had for a long time," wrote a Virginia lady to her son. "I must take advantage of it. *Thank God*, I have almost gotten thro' Christmas. What a slave a holiday makes of a mistress! Indeed, she is always a slave, but doubly and trebly so at such times." [23]

Plantation wives did not work in the field as did wives of small farmers but many did their own spinning, weaving, and sewing. The son of a small slaveholder in the Colleton district of South Carolina recalled that

my mother spun, wove cloth, cooked and occasionally went to the cow pen to milk the cows, father plowed and drove the wagon, made shoes and did other work. My mother always seed to her cooking and did a good deal of it, had her spinning and weaving done for the whole plantation white and black, no cloth or negro shoes were bought whilst father and mother lived, father made his own negro shoes and mother made the clothes.[24]

On one farm in a moment of crisis when the mother and all the children were ill, a Negro slave rejected in bewilderment the suggestion that he milk the cow, on the ground that everybody knew that to be "woman's work" and therefore impossible for him to undertake.[25]

22. James C. Bonner, ed., "Plantation Experiences of a New York Woman," *North Carolina Historical Review* 33 (July 1956): 384–412.

23. L. Minor Blackford, *Mine Eyes Have Seen the Glory* (Cambridge, Mass., 1954), p. 7, quoting his grandmother Lucy Carter Minor.

24. David Gavin Diary, 31 May 1865, SHC UNC.

25. A Southern Country Minister, *Old Pine Farm* (Nashville: Southwestern Publishing House, 1860), pp. 93–94. This is an unusual book in that it depicts, apparently autobiographically, the life of a minister's family living in a log cabin with two slaves. Its author intended, he says, to "show up some of the features of Southern Ministerial life among the country churches." His livelihood came, of course, not from his preaching but from the farm.

No matter how large or wealthy the establishment, the mistress was expected to understand not only the skills of spinning, weaving, and sewing but also gardening, care of poultry, care of the sick, and all aspects of food preparation from the sowing of seed to the appearance of the final product on the table. Fine ladies thought nothing of supervising hog butchering on the first cold days in fall, or of drying fruits and vegetables for the winter. They made their own yeast, lard, and soap, set their own hens, and were expected to be able to make with equal skill a rough dress for a slave or a ball gown for themselves. It was customary for the mistress to rise at five or six, and to be in the kitchen when the cook arrived, to "overlook" all the arrangements for the day. A Virginia gentleman's bland assertion that "a considerable portion of her life must be spent in the nursery and the sickroom" [26] was a simple description of reality. The view that illness was inevitable was suggested in a diary entry of a Vicksburg woman, mother of a new baby: "I have felt rather depressed this evening, fearing a long summer of heat & sickness—even if I keep well how can I nurse baby and my sick too?" [27]

Even extraordinary wealth could not buy leisure for a planter's wife. Thomas Dabney owned a thousand acres and five hundred slaves, and until the Civil War was one of the wealthiest men in Mississippi. His wife bore sixteen children, carried on all the normal responsibilities of a plantation mistress, and moved her large menage of children and house slaves to the Gulf coast each summer.[28] The childless

26. Thomas R. Dew in the *Southern Literary Messenger* 1 (May 1835): 497.

27. Diary of Mahala P. Roach, 15 May 1859, typescript, SHC UNC.

28. Smedes, *Memorials,* passim.

mistress of a rich Roanoke River plantation combined
wine-making, peach-pruning, canning, and gardening with
reading, study, and assistance to her husband. It was her
custom to ride over their various plantations with him, and
to keep his account books. In 1860 she promised herself "by
energy and self-denial and strict attenion to detail to master
this debt." [29]

A South Carolina matron recorded, somewhat breath-
lessly:

A Plantation life is a very active one. This morning I got up
late having been disturbed in the night, hurried down to have
something arranged for breakfast, Ham & eggs, . . . wrote a
letter to Charles . . . had prayers, got the boys off to town.
Had work cut out, gave orders about dinner, had the horse feed
fixed in hot water, had the box filled with cork: went to see
about the carpenters working at the negro houses. . . . these
carpenters Mr. Grimball told me he wished me to see about
every day, & now I have to cut out the flannel jackets.[30]

She does not indicate how she found time to keep a diary in
addition.

A middle Georgia matron supervised a milk dairy, a loom
house, and a meat house, as well as a large poultry yard in
which she included geese for feather beds. Withal she bore
eleven children and raised nine to maturity.[31]

An Alabama planter's wife described her days in a laconic
diary:

October 20, 1859. Put in quilt for Olivia
        Oct. 21st. Spent the day in quilting. Some hog
                    drovers spent the night here.

29. Edmonston, "Diary of Looking Glass Plantation," 13 July 1860.
30. Meta Morris Grimball Diary, 29 December 1860, SHC UNC.
31. Felton, *Country Life in Georgia,* p. 29.

Nov. 2. Preparing a web of cloth for the
loom. . . .

Nov. 5. Went to Yellow Creek. Mr. Flood
preached on the election and did his
subject credit I thought.

Dec. 7. This has been a busy day. We slaugh-
tered 15 hogs, large ones. It is my
birthday and I sit this evening by a
fire, recording the fact—44 I have seen

Dec. 8. . . . I dried up 22 gallons of lard

Dec. 10. . . . finished our sausage, made up and
to press some cheese souse.[32]

The work of town-dwelling women was very much like
that of their country cousins, except that there were fewer
slaves to supervise. A doctor's wife in Salisbury, North
Carolina, administered the equivalent of a small farm
within the city limits and "a home unit of industry to carry
on all those processes which are now delegated to the baker,
the grocer, and a dozen other trades."[33] Similarly, the
widow of a United States senator living on six acres in
Columbia, South Carolina, supervised all the work inside
and outside the house, taught sewing to slave girls and her
own daughters, and carried the responsibility for a plantation in the country as well.[34] The wife of a Vicksburg
railroad official sewed continually and was so burdened with
household cares that she felt guilty about sitting in the
parlor talking to guests unless she had sewing in her hands.

32. Private Journal of Mrs. Sarah R. Espy, 20 October 1859. Alabama
Department of Archives, quoted in M. C. Boyd, *Alabama in the Fifties*
(New York: Columbia University Press, 1931), pp. 116–18.

33. Hope Summerell Chamberlain, *This Was Home* (Chapel Hill:
University of North Carolina Press, 1938), p. 43.

34. Grace Elmore Diary, typescript, vol. 2, Covering 1864–65, passim,
SHC UNC.

She, too, planted her own garden, took up carpets in the spring, cooked and washed, and cared for children, despite the fact that she was never without house slaves. The indefatigable Mrs. Grimball showed no more sign of taking her ease during her winter sojourns in Charleston than in her summer ones on the plantation.[35]

From the earliest settlement of the South some women had been planters in their own right. In 1807 a pioneer in the Louisiana territory reported upon returning from a trip east: "I found my family well and my Plantation affairs better conducted than if I had been at home. Mrs. B. has acquired a high reputation as a cotton planter." [36] Another Louisiana woman took full charge of a plantation because her husband was a surveyor and often away from home, and many wives of professional men or politicians were part-time planters. Congressman Clement Clay, Sr., of Alabama took it for granted that his wife would make plantation decisions when he was in Washington, and when he finally decided that he wanted her with him it was she who wrote letters home to overseers and relatives to make sure that all the details were attended to.[37]

The skill with which many widows carried on plantations suggests that women knew a good deal more about the planting operation than has generally been supposed. A widow in Wilkinson County, Louisiana, ran a plantation from the time her husband died until her son was old

35. Mahala P. Roach Diary and Meta Morris Grimball Diary, passim, SHC UNC.

36. David Bradford Papers, 30 November 1807, Dept. of Archives, LSU.

37. Mrs. Andrew McCollum Diary, SHC UNC; C. C. Clay Papers, MS Dept., Duke; Ruth Ketring Nuremberger, *The Clays of Alabama* (Lexington: University of Kentucky Press, 1958).

enough to assume responsibility. Her correspondence with a New Orleans factor is filled with careful detail and astute negotiation.[38] Another young widow moved to Louisiana, bought land, and established a profitable sugar plantation, while she carried on all the normal duties of a plantation wife as well.[39] When a South Carolina planter died toward the end of the war his widow "suddenly had to plan and arrange for the 100 people on the farms in North Carolina, as well as for the 500 down on the plantations. It was perfectly wonderful to see how she rose to the requirements of the moment, and how strong and level her mind was." [40]

The belief that woman was created to be a wife and mother did not allow much room for spinsters, but of course there were some. In the families of yeoman farmers, single women performed agricultural labor and, according to the manuscript census returns, sometimes owned and operated farms independently.[41] Others hired out to do housework or sewed for more prosperous neighbors. Women of all classes sold surplus produce, and some ran millinery shops and bakeshops, inns and boardinghouses, as well as small schools. By the 1850s travelers commented on the fact that a few white girls were working in small cotton mills in Augusta, Athens, and Graniteville—a slight forecast of the future. A spinster of good family had very few options. Even if she had money of her own, respectability required a family, so she was apt to live with relatives, performing

38. Nancy Pinson Papers, Dept. of Archives, LSU; see also Diary of Sarah Witherspoon Erwin McIver, Coker Papers, SHC UNC, and the collection of papers of women planters at LSU.

39. *Brockenburn: The Journal of Kate Stone,* ed. John Q. Anderson (Baton Rouge: Louisiana State University Press, 1955).

40. Pringle, *Chronicles of Chicora Wood,* p. 212.

41. Owsley, *Plain Folk,* pp. 11–13.

unpaid labor in return for the requisite social sanction. A woman with no such home available might go out as governess or housekeeper, though the average wage of four dollars a month which prevailed in North Carolina just before the Civil War could not have been a great incentive. Not all incentives were monetary, however. One North Carolina woman, an orphan, consulted friends and relatives about the propriety of taking such a housekeeper's job in a widower's family. A few months later she married her employer and eventually bore him a dozen children.[42]

Few aspects of women's work accorded so poorly with the image of delicate, frivolous, submissive women than the responsibility for managing slaves. Slavery influenced the lives and thoughts of southern women in many ways, not least in the kinds of work it created. Supervising slaves was difficult, demanding, frustrating, and above all never-ending. The wife allocated duties among house servants, who on a large plantation might number dozens of slaves. In addition the mistress was often responsible for dealing out weekly rations to all the slaves, and for making sure that they were clothed according to the standards of her plantation.

The mistress was usually chief medical officer, responsible for the health of family and slaves, and for the delivery of babies. On a large plantation someone was nearly always sick, and epidemics were not infrequent. The fertility of slave women was economically important to the master, but it added to the burdens of the mistress. One plantation wife recorded every few days the birth of a slave child over which she had presided.[43]

42. Lucy Cole Burwell Papers, MS Dept., Duke; for the $4 wage see Guion G. Johnson, *Ante-Bellum North Carolina* (Chapel Hill: University of North Carolina Press, 1937), p. 247.

43. Sarah McIver Diary, SHC UNC.

Supervising slaves raised problems of controlling and guiding behavior. The mistress had to dispense justice, settle small personal feuds, and cajole those who did not want to work into doing so. Women gifted in human relations had little difficulty and their household affairs ran smoothly even when there was much work to be done. Others, less gifted, had constant problems with /recalcitrant, defiant, slovenly slaves, some of whom were skilled at intimidating their mistresses. Such personal relationships ran the gamut from that typified by one diary note, "Business negligently done & much altogether neglected, some disobedience, much idleness, sulleness, slovenliness. . . . Used the rod," to those of the warm, peaceful Smedes household, based upon Mrs. Smedes's injunction to her daughters, "They are not machines, they are just like you, made from the same flesh and blood." [44]

One of the most persistent threads in the romanticization of woman was the glorification of motherhood, with its great possibilities for beneficent influence on the coming generation. Nothing in the myth emphasized the darker side of maternity. In the face of the idealization of the family and the aura of sanctity surrounding the word "mother," only in private could women give voice to the misery of endless pregnancies, with attendant illness, and the dreadful fear of childbirth, a fear based on fact. The number of women who died in childbirth was high. When the mother survived the family tended to be large. "Family on the increase continually, and every one added increased labor and responsibility. And this was the case with the typical southern

44. Lucilla McCorkle Diary, 5 July 1846, SHC UNC; Smedes, *Memorials*, p. 88. The relation of women and slaves is discussed more fully in the following chapter.

woman," wrote one upper-class wife.[45] "My heart almost sinks within me at the thought of feeding another child," a pregnant woman wrote her mother.[46] "I have never been so opposed to having children as many women I know," wrote a Georgia woman discussing her husband's objection to any further increase in the family, and inadvertently throwing light on the views of her friends.[47]

The depth of the fear of pregnancy came out clearly in much husband-wife correspondence. "Please let me know if your hopes as to your condition the day you left Richmond turned out to be as you thought or if it was a false alarm," wrote General William Dorsey Pender to his wife, who had just spent seven weeks with him in camp. "I sincerely hope it was bona fide, for we all have enough to contend with in these times even when we are free from continuous nausea and do not have to look forward to nine months of pain and general ill feeling." And, a year later, "Indeed I did sincerely hope that you had escaped this time, but darling it must be the positive and direct will of God that it should be so." Notwithstanding this pious observation, he enclosed some pills which the camp surgeon thought might bring on a spontaneous abortion.[48]

A North Carolina planter's wife found constant child-bearing such a trial that she began making longer and longer visits to her own family, to the point, finally, that her husband ordered her to come home. Her unhappiness at the

45. V. V. Clayton, *White and Black under the Old Regime* (Milwaukee: Young Churchmen Co., 1899), p. 124.

46. Laura Norwood to Mrs. L. L. Lenoir, 1 May 1845, Lenoir Papers, SHC UNC.

47. E. G. Thomas Diary 29 November 1870, MS Dept., Duke. See also Johnson, *Ante-Bellum North Carolina*, p. 237.

48. Hassler, ed., *The General to His Lady*, p. 114, 21 February 1862, and ibid., p. 202, 10 March 1863.

thought of frequent pregnancy did not diminish, and in 1862 when he went off to one of the Virginia springs for his health she wrote that her only hope was to die young: "Some wifes are nothing but trouble, and I am one, I'm not fit for anything but to have children, and that is nothing but trouble and sorrow." Her wish for early death was not granted, and in 1867 when he went to the legislature she was still worrying: "Willis, I have not seen anything of my monthlies yet, and I am afraid your going to Raleigh and coming home will make me suffer. . . . you know I hate even to think of such a thing." To which he unfeelingly replied, "I was never hopeful that you would not have more children, you come of a breed too prolific to stop at your age and if its the Lords will why we must submit to it." [49] This after thirteen years of marriage.

The absence of effective contraception created a strain on the domestic relationship. This, more than a commitment to ladylike decorum, may have been responsible for the widespread but erroneous view that eroticism was a thing unknown among southern ladies. Sensitive men felt the strain. General Pender tried to become a Christian in order to control "my stumbling block in this world. . . . I do feel humbled and mortified to think that the most dangerous of all our passions and the most sinful when indulged in, should be the one I cannot conquer." [50] When one of the Alabama Clays came home after long and much-deplored absence at war his wife was soon pregnant with her eleventh

49. Willis Williams to his wife Harriet, 18 January 1858; Harriet Williams to Willis Williams, 23 October 1862; same to same 26 January 1867; Willis Williams to Harriet Williams, 31 January 1867, all in Willis Williams Papers, SHC UNC.

50. Hassler, ed., *The General to His Lady,* pp. 57–58, 11 September 1861.

child. Both husband and wife, so his brother commented, looked on the event with "grief and regret." [51]

Given the handicaps under which women suffered, the surprising thing is not that so many marriages were miserable, but that so many were happy over long periods of time. "God bless my precious husband and keep him at my side as long as I live is my prayer. His forty-sixth birthday. We grow older but age only brings an increase of affection. We have joyed and sorrowed together for twenty-three years" wrote a Georgia planter's wife.[52] "Thank God for the unity of spirit which exists between Patrick and myself. I do not believe I could live had I not him to lean on and confide in. He is the only person to whom I ever . . . unburden myself fully." [53] "How comfortable! How great a happiness to have a companion, a partner of all joys & woes in whom entire confidence can be placed." [54] "I cannot close my reminiscences without paying your father a most inadequate tribute. I have no words to do him justice. I can only say he was my guide, my inspiration, a man of the purest heart, loftiest aspirations, who tried to do his duty." [55] "You will call me a silly woman when I tell you that I was so delighted to receive your letter of September 20 that I laughingly kissed it." [56] "Tomorrow will be thirteen years since my marriage. How swiftly time has flown and how full of happiness have these years been to me. I thank God for his goodness and mercy towards us as a family." [57] "This March

51. C. C. Clay Papers, MS Dept., Duke.
52. Josephine Clay Habersham, *Ebb Tide* (Athens, Ga., 1958), p. 52.
53. Edmonston, "Diary of Looking Glass Plantation," 17 March 1861.
54. Diary of Fannie Moore Webb Bumpas, 9 March 1842, SHC UNC.
55. Katherine Polk Gale, "Recollections," SHC UNC.
56. Mrs. E. J. Warren to her husband, 21 September 1866, SHC UNC.
57. Susan Cornwall Shewmake Journal, 1 March 1861, SHC UNC.

we have been married 31 years and is this not a cause for thankfulness. Here is a man . . . very much in love with his wife of 51 years and, although not in robust health, getting on, more amiable than he was." [58] "I would give anything to be near you or with you," wrote Rachel Cheves, separated from her husband by the war; he replied, "Whatever befalls, you are more dear to me than ever, if it were possible I would go in quest of you." [59]

From other men came the authentic voice of romantic love which had survived years of marriage. W. H. Bagley, writing to his wife in 1869, waxed poetic, "Being away from you makes me feel *how* absolutely dear to me you are, and what a necessity to my happiness. . . . Everything tells me I am away from you." [60] A Methodist minister struck the same note: "You say I am very dear to you, you are, *my lovely one,* increasingly dear to me. Absence from you is more painful to me than ever, and I feel an increasing concern for you, under the heavy responsibilities that fall on you in my absence." [61] Another, less affluent minister, after a family financial crisis in which his wife had taken hold of things, wrote, "Who can estimate the worth of such a woman? . . . God's richest blessing be upon the hopeful, truthful, Christian wife." [62]

What in retrospect may seem to have been intolerable

58. Meta Morris Grimball Diary, February 1861, SHC UNC. Mrs. Grimball could hardly guess that her husband would live to be ninety-two.

59. J. R. Cheves Papers, 27 February 1865, 2 March 1865, MS Dept., Duke.

60. W. H. Bagley to Addie Worth Bagley, 11 August 1869, Worth Papers, SHC UNC.

61. Joseph Davis to his wife Anne, 28 April 1847, Beale-Davis Papers, SHC UNC.

62. A Southern Country Minister, *Old Pine Farm,* p. 160.

strains on family relationships were thought by their victims to be the natural, if somewhat harsh, order of the universe. There was no experience to suggest that things might be different. But while there were mismatches and misery aplenty, there were also happy families, sometimes, indeed, very happy families.

If the inwardness of the man-woman relationships can only be guessed at, other things about the realities of the domestic world are clear. For most southern women the domestic circle *was* the world. Girls married young, and might go on having children for thirty years. Courtship and love affairs supplied much of the excitement in a relatively uneventful rural society, but marriages were as often as not pragmatically or even casually contracted and in any case romance gave way almost at once to practical things.

For most women life was narrow and provincial. Communications were poor; in many places the mail came once a week, perhaps to a distant post office. In a thinly settled country one day was pretty much like another. Women could speak of being confined to the house "until spring" by bad weather and sickly children. Life quite naturally centered on family, and letters are filled with detailed reports on uncles, aunts, parents, and children. Health was of great concern; nearly every letter began with a careful account of the state of health of each member of the family and thanks to God when it was good. The general health of the community and a list of recent deaths were also staples of correspondence.

Religion provided a good deal of interest. Revivals, lengthy meetings, and "love feasts"—one day revivals— bulked large in otherwise uneventful times. The state of one's soul, and of the souls of recently deceased neighbors, was a subject for reporting to friends.

Visiting was the essence of life. It filled the need for stimulation now accomplished by newspapers, radio, television, movies, daily mail, and a thousand other distractions. In towns even busy men spent some part of the day calling on friends, and in the country visits from family or friends were usually overnight and might—in the case of maiden aunts or widowed parents—stretch on for weeks or months. The conversation, so far as it has been recorded, dwelt heavily on personal topics, with religion running a close second. The relationships between young women and young men were of great interest, especially to the parties themselves, and there was much open expression of affection.

In Charleston and New Orleans, or on a great landed estate here and there, a more cosmopolitan society existed. Wealthy people could travel, buy new books, subscribe to English reviews, and meet their counterparts in Newport or Saratoga or Paris. For the majority, life was simple, demanding, limited to domestic excitements, and quite self-contained.[63]

Within this framework the southern family lived and developed its pattern of existence. Family ties were strong, and even the great mobility of the westward movement did not always diminish them. Whole families including cousins and more than one generation might move together, one member going ahead to reconnoiter and the whole clan

63. The contrast between the cosmopolitan society of Charleston and Columbia and the provinciality of plantation life is a theme running through the whole of Mrs. Chesnut's remarkable diary. See especially her comparisons of life in Washington and life on her father-in-law's plantation. *Diary from Dixie,* pp. 3, 10, 24, 26, 34, 41, 165–67, and passim.

coming after. Or if one branch moved west and another remained in the east, there would be regular letters and visits. After Thomas Dabney moved to Mississippi, he made an annual pilgrimage to see his mother in Virginia, taking a different one of his sixteen children each year.

The real life of the southern lady was more varied and more demanding than the fantasies of southern men would suggest. She became, as the myth assured her she must, a wife and mother as soon as the opportunity offered. Thereafter she was likely to work hard for the rest of her life, having a baby every year or so, developing in the process of her experience a steely self-control, and the knowledge that the work she did was essential gave meaning to her life. Few people ever asked her if she thought life was as it ought to be, and usually only in indirect and private ways did she raise the question herself.

"Have you asked her whether
  she is satisfied . . . ?"
[An imaginary husband speaks]
"No, but I know she is. She
is too amiable to desire what
would make me unhappy, and
too judicious to wish to step
beyond the sphere of her sex.
I will never consent to have our
  peace disturbed by such
  discussions."

Margaret Fuller,
Woman in the Nineteenth Century

3

Discontent

Open complaint about their lot was not the custom among southern ladies; yet their contented acceptance of the home as the "sphere to which God had appointed them" was sometimes more apparent than real. Most southern women would not have tried, or known how, to free themselves from the system which was supposed to be divinely ordained, but there is considerable evidence that many of them found the "sphere" very confining.

Women's expressions of unhappiness centered in two principal areas of life. One was their relationship to slaves. This complex web encompassed marriage, family life, and sexual mores as these were defined by the patriarchal doctrine. The second area of constant concern was education. Many women felt deeply deprived because their opportunities for learning were so limited.

For women, as for men, slaves were a troublesome property. It was not only that the administration of a large establishment was complex and demanding, or even that the mistress was expected to be a combination of supervisor, teacher, doctor, and minister to a large family of slaves. The greatest burden was psychological, of being day in and day out the arbiter of so many relationships, the person upon whom so many human beings depended. There was no privacy. "These women," Mrs. Chesnut wrote, ". . . have less chance to live their own lives than if they were African missionaries. They have a swarm of blacks about them like children under their care . . . and they hate slavery worse than Mrs. Stowe does."[1]

Such conditions were bound to breed antagonism toward slaves. The expressions of it were common in diaries and

1. *Diary from Dixie,* p. 163.

letters, right through the Civil War. "I wish I could for once see a hearty negro woman who admitted herself to be over 40, one who was not 'poorly, Thank God.!' To be 'poorly' is their aim and object, as it ends in the house and spinning." [2] "I cannot, nor will not, spend all these precious days of my life following after and watching Negroes. It is a terrible life!" [3] "We contemplate removing to a free state. There we hope to be relieved of many unpleasant things, but particularly of the evils of slavery, for slaves are a continual source of trouble. . . . They are a source of more trouble to housewives than all other things, vexing them and causing much sin." [4] "I sometimes think I would not care if they all did go, they are so much trouble to me." [5] "When we change our residence, I cast my vote for a free state. . . . Negroes are nothing but a tax and annoyance to their owners." [6] "The negroes are a weight continually pulling us down! Will the time *ever* come for us to be free of them?" [7] "Mr. Dunbar's Joe left Monday. He was a consummate hypocrite, in fact they all are." [8]

Antagonism was only one part of the picture. There was also affection. It is possible to jettison nine-tenths of the sentiment about Negro mammies and still have substantial evidence of what was not, after all, a surprising phenomenon. Women who lived and worked together often formed bonds of friendship and mutual dependency across the color

2. Catherine Edmonston, "Diary of Looking Glass Plantation," December 1860.

3. Laura Beecher Comer Diary, 5 January 1862, SHC UNC.

4. Fannie Moore Webb Bumpas Diary, 15 August 1843, SHC UNC.

5. Catherine Barbara Broun Diary, 1 January 1864, SHC UNC.

6. Diary of Mrs. Isaac Hilliard, 16 and 19 June 1850, Dept. of Archives, LSU.

7. Letitia M. Burwell, *Girl's Life,* p. 61.

8. Anonymous Diary, 30 July 1866, MS Dept., Duke.

bar. "An affectionate friendship that was to last for more than sixty years," one man wrote of his mother and a slave. "She was a member of the family," wrote a Mississippi woman, and another, "She loved me devotedly and I was much attached to her." [9] A visiting Englishman commented upon the close relationship between the Calhoun ladies and their slaves. [10]

In the end antagonism and love led to the same conclusion: slavery was an evil. Most southern women who expressed themselves on the peculiar institution opposed slavery and were glad when it was ended. Mrs. Chesnut quoted her friend and confidante Isabella Martin as saying she never saw a true woman who was not an abolitionist, and Mrs. Chesnut herself claimed to have been one from the age of nineteen. The motives for antislavery feelings were mixed. Susan Dabney Smedes, describing her grandmother's abolitionism, was unable to say whether those sentiments were based on "sympathy with the colored race or with their owners." [11] Whatever the motive, expressions of antislavery feelings ran through many personal documents.

"I must say that my mother never did like slavery and did not hesitate to say so. Her father once sent her a present of ten slaves which she sent back." [12] "In some mysterious way I had drunk in with my mother's milk . . . a detestation of the curse of slavery laid upon our beautiful southern

9. L. Minor Blackford, *Mine Eyes Have Seen the Glory*, p. 48; Susan Dabney Smedes, *Memorials of a Southern Planter*, pp. 47–48; V. V. Clayton, *White and Black under the Old Regime*, p. 127.

10. G. W. Featherstonhaugh, *A Canoe Voyage up the Minnay Sotor* (London, 1847), quoted in K. Jones, *Plantation South*, p. 127.

11. *Memorials*, p. 82. *Diary from Dixie*, passim. The theme of women as abolitionists runs through the diary.

12. Reminiscences of E. V. J. Semple, SHC UNC, p. 18.

land." [13] "Had slavery lasted a few years longer, I have heard my mother say, it would have killed Julia, my head-woman, and me. Our burden of work and responsibility was simply staggering. . . .. I was glad and thankful—on my own account when slavery ended, and I ceased to belong body and soul to my negroes. As my mother said, so said other southern mistresses." [14] "I often said to my husband that the freedom of the Negroes was a freedom to me." [15] "I do not see how I can live my life amid these people! . . . To be always among people whom I do not understand and whom I must guide, and teach and lead on like children. It frightens me." [16] "I wish we could get rid of all [slaves] at their value and leave this wretched country. I am more and more convinced that it is no place to rear a family of children." [17] "[I could not see] how the men I most honored and admired, my husband among the rest [,] could constantly justify it, and not only that but say that it was a blessing to the slave." [18] Years later a Louisiana woman wrote that she had been "subject at all times to the exactions and dictations of the black people who belonged to me, which now seems too extraordinary and incredible to relate." [19] "All my family on both sides . . . were slave

13. Constance Cary Harrison, *Recollections Grave and Gay* (London: Smith, Elder, 1912), p. 42.

14. Myrta L. Avary, *Dixie after the War* (New York: D. Appleton, 1903), pp. 179–81.

15. V. V. Clayton, *White and Black,* p. 155.

16. Elizabeth Allston Pringle, *Chronicles of Chicora Wood,* p. 66.

17. Anna Matilda King to Thomas Butler King, December 1844, SHC UNC.

18. Cornelia McDonald, *A Diary with Reminiscences of the War and Refugee Life in the Shenendoah Valley* (Nashville: Cullom & Ghertner, 1935), pp. 11–12.

19. Caroline Merrick, *Old Times in Dixie Land* (New York: Grafton Press, 1901), pp. 17–18.

owners . . . but I do not hesitate to say that slavery was a curse to the South." [20] "I was born and raised in the South . . . as were all my relations before me. . . . Yet . . . my first recollection is of pity for the Negroes and desire to help them. . . . Always I felt the moral guilt of it, felt how impossible it must be for an owner of slaves to win his way into Heaven." [21] "Southern women are all, I believe, abolitionists." [22]

In the spring of 1855 Charles Eliot Norton visited friends in Charleston. Writing to James Russell Lowell on Good Friday of that year he reflected:

> It is a very strange thing to hear men of character and cultivation . . . expressing their belief in open fallacies and monstrous principles [e.g., the defense of slavery]. . . . It seems to me sometimes as if only the women here read the New Testament, and as if the men regarded Christianity rather as a gentlemanly accomplishment than as anything more serious. It is very different with the women . . . but they are bewildered often, and their efforts are limited by weakness, inexperience, and opposition. Their eyes fill with tears when you talk with them about it.[23]

A number of women saw a parallel between their own situation and that of slaves, a comparison made too often to be counted simply as rhetoric. "There is no slave, after all, like a wife," Mary Chesnut wrote in a bitter moment. Or,

---

20. Rebecca Latimer Felton, *The Subjection and Enfranchisement of Women,* pamphlet, MS Dept., University of Georgia.

21. *Brockenburn: The Journal of Kate Stone,* pp. 6–8.

22. E. G. C. Thomas Diary, 2 January, 1859, MS Dept., Duke.

23. Sara Norton and Mark A. DeWolfe Howe, *Letters of Charles Eliot Norton, with Biographical Comment* (Boston: Houghton Mifflin, 1913), 1: 126–27. I am indebted to Mr. Ralph Luker for calling this letter to my attention.

"You know how women sell themselves and are sold in marriage, from queens downward. . . . Poor women, poor slaves." And yet again, "All married women, all children and girls who live in their father's houses are slaves." [24] "It was a saying that the mistress of a plantation was the most complete slave on it." [25]

Perhaps it was understanding growing from this identification with slaves which led so many southern women to be private abolitionists, and even a few to be public ones. Of the latter Sarah and Angelina Grimké were the most striking. Sarah was from childhood rebellious against the lot of southern women and fought throughout her adult life for the emancipation of women and slaves. Angelina also worked to free the slaves, married a leading abolitionist, and in her *Appeal to the Christian Women of the South* addressed herself to the parallels between the experiences of women and of slaves.[26]

Mary Berkeley Minor Blackford was another southern woman who took her discontent with slavery to the world. A Virginian of bluest blood and a busy housewife with six children, she spent her spare time and money, as well as all the money she could charm from her friends, buying slaves to be sent to freedom in Liberia. Although the colonization movement was regarded by radical abolitionists as a refuge for people unwilling to face the true dimensions of the slavery question, Mrs. Blackford's diagnosis of the ills of slavery was radical enough:

24. *Diary from Dixie,* pp. 49 and 486.
25. Smedes, *Memorials,* p. 179.
26. Gerda Lerner, *The Grimké Sisters* (Boston: Houghton Mifflin, 1967), pp. 21 ff. A more detailed discussion of Sarah Grimké in a different context appears on pp. 61–63 below.

Think what it is to be a Slave!!! To be treated not as a man but as a personal chattel, a thing that may be *bought* and *sold,* to have *no right* to the fruits of your own labour, *no right* to your own wife and children, liable at any moment to be seperated [*sic*] at the arbitrary will of another from all that is dearest to you on earth, & whom it is your duty to love & cherish. Deprived by the law of learning to read the Bible, compelled to know that the purity of your wife and daughters is exposed without protection of law to the assault of a brutal white man! Think of this, and all the nameless horrors that are concentrated in that one word *Slavery.*[27]

The evils of slavery tended to merge with the grievances, even the repressed grievances, of southern women. The slave was deprived of a secure family life, had to obey his master, and in some states was denied by law the right to learn. For women, family life had its quota of pain, much of it related to slavery, and they, too, were supposed to take orders from men and to learn only so much as would not unfit them for their appropriate role in the patriarchy.

The virtues of this domestic system, which men praised so highly, were not always clear to their subordinates in the hierarchy. "Under slavery we live surrounded by prostitutes," wrote Mary Chesnut; "like patriarchs of old, our men live in one house with their wives and concubines. . . . Any lady is ready to tell you who is the father of all the mulatto children in everybody's household but her own." This theme runs through her diary:

A magnate who runs a hideous black harem with its consequences under the same roof with his lovely white wife, and his beautiful accomplished daughters . . . poses as the model of all human virtues to these poor women whom God and the laws

27. Blackford, *Mine Eyes Have Seen the Glory,* p. 47.

have given him. From the height of his awful majesty, he scolds and thunders at them, as if he never did wrong in his life.[28]

Few southern women appreciated the argument of a South Carolina gentleman who thought the availability of slave women avoided the horrors of prostitution. He pointed out that men could satisfy their sexual needs while increasing their slave property.[29] The bitterness of southern women on this subject came out again and again. One spoke of "violations of the moral law that made mulattoes as common as blackberries," and suggested that the four years of bloody war was a fit penance for so many sins.[30] "I saw slavery in its bearing on my sex," wrote another. "I saw that it teemed with injustice and shame to all womankind and I hated it."[31]

There was an undercurrent of concern about venereal disease. The fiction women wrote and read was full of mysteriously disillusioned brides and dissolute men. A North Carolina student in the 1840s could remark without comment that the university was "never free from clap." Conversely, the exaggerated praise heaped upon "pure" men reflected something more than admiration of good character. It was an index to the anxiety of women endangered by their husbands. Primitive medical knowledge offered little protection to the wives of men whose visits to the slave quarters left them diseased.

28. *Diary from Dixie,* pp. 21–22.
29. Chancellor Harper, "Memoir on Slavery," *Southern Literary Journal,* February 1838, p. 1.
30. Rebecca Latimer Felton, *Country Life in Georgia, in the Days of My Youth,* p. 79.
31. Elizabeth Lyle Saxon, *A Southern Woman's Wartime Reminiscences* (privately printed, 1905), p. 14.

Chapter three

Miscegenation was only one grievance. Women felt deeply aggrieved by the prevailing double standard. The conventions of nineteenth-century discourse make precise evidence difficult to come by, but veiled comments suggest that many women found the social standards governing sexual life hard to accept. The accepted belief was that only men and depraved women were sexual creatures and that pure women were incapable of erotic feeling. The inadequacy of this description is made apparent in fiction, biography, personal documents, and court records.

The syrupy descriptions of romantic love nearly always carried erotic overtones, and the constant emphasis upon woman's "magic spell," indicated something about the unconscious preoccupations of the society. A Methodist minister thought it self-evident that puberty was the period when "the female, pressed by a new want . . . should renounce that inexperience in love which was becoming in tranquil youth," [32] should, in other words, begin to think of marriage. "The villain . . . had at length found the unguarded moment in which a woman can deny nothing to the man she loves," said one of Beverly Tucker's characters.[33] A college boy expressing horror at the rumor of Daniel Webster's marital infidelities also noted (possibly from his own observation but more likely from student gossip) that "women of late have become unfaithful to their husbands. Some women I don't believe can be satisfied." Mrs. Chesnut recorded premarital as well as extramarital sex among her friends and acquaintances and the historian of antebellum North Carolina found many respected citizens asking the legislature to

32. John C. Bayley, *Marriage As It Is and Should Be,* p. 14.
33. *George Balcombe,* 1: 63.

legitimize their bastard children.[34] Angelina Grimké, whose ideas on the subject began to be formed in Charleston, in a letter to her fiancé threw light on the sexual scene:

I have been tempted to think marriage was *sinful,* because of what appeared to me almost invariably to prompt and lead to it. Instead of the higher, nobler sentiments being first aroused, and leading on the lower passions *captive* to their will, the *latter* seemed to be *lords* over the former. Well I am convinced that men in general, the vast majority, believe most seriously that women were made to gratify their animal appetites.[35]

The evidence does not bear out the notion that all the good women, all the respectable wives, totally suppressed their sexuality, though the values of their society certainly encouraged them to do so. It suggests instead a bitterness against the freedom which men arrogated to themselves and the restrictions they laid upon women. Mrs. Chesnut quoted one Charleston matron:

Now I assert that the theory upon which modern society is based is all wrong. A man is supposed to confide his honor to his wife. If she misbehaves herself, his honor is tarnished. But how can a man be disgraced by another person's doing what, if he did it himself . . . he would not be hurt at all in public estimation? [36]

A Georgia woman commented upon a friend who had left her husband when she discovered him to be supporting a

34. John L. Sanders, ed., "Diary of Ruffin Wirt Tomlinson," *North Carolina Historical Review* 30 (January–April 1953): 243; Guion Johnson, *Ante-Bellum North Carolina,* pp. 209–10.

35. Gilbert Barnes and Dwight L. Dumond, eds., *Letters of Theodore Dwight Weld, Angelina Grimké Weld, and Sarah Grimké 1822–1844* (New York: D. Appleton-Century, 1934), 2: 587.

36. Chesnut, *Diary from Dixie,* p. 224.

mistress and a second family. She approved the woman's courage, adding, "I do think she would have been doing an injustice to herself to remain with him—yet how often this is done—How often let Martyr women testify!" She went on to discuss another case in which a married woman had run away with another man, saying that the husband would be considered quite justified if he refused to take her back, while the other man's wife would of course be expected to receive her wayward spouse without comment. "Custom does indeed sanction many a wrong. But I mount my hobby horse when I converse on the subject of woman and her wrongs." [37]

Some discreet Charleston ladies appeared to manage their affairs without disgrace, but the theory was that one misstep ruined a woman forever. The diary of a well-educated and intelligent New Orleans concubine made it clear that while she was seeking counsel from a minister and hoping for God's forgiveness, she accepted without question the fact that the local community would not forgive her. [38] In a popular novel a beautiful and capable "good" girl put herself beyond the pale in one half-hour, in her own eyes as well as those of a would-be suitor. [39]

There were still other reasons, besides miscegenation and the double standard, for a good deal of well-concealed misery in marriage. Oscar Handlin has suggested that the increase in life expectancy in the nineteenth century, preced-

37. E. G. C. Thomas Diary, 1858.
38. Diary of Madeline Selina Edwards, SHC UNC. Ironically, when she was deserted by her lover and forced to earn money she tried writing articles for magazines on "domestic happiness."
39. Tucker, *George Balcombe,* 1: 53–60.

ing as it did the widespread understanding of contraception, increased the strain on domestic tranquility.[40] Earlier, in the eighteenth century, the high mortality rate made it possible for some persons to marry three or four times. If one marriage was unsuccessful, the next might be better. By the 1830s, however, when the glorification of family life and domestic joy was at its peak, declining death rates increased the liklihood of having to live a whole lifetime with the same mate.

Even in happy marriages, patriarchal assumptions could cause some chafing. Mary Chesnut admired her husband and enjoyed his company, yet her comments on men in general and James Chesnut in particular were frequently acerb: "What a blessed humbug domestic felicity is, eh? . . . But he is master of the house. To hear is to obey. . . . all the comfort of my life depends upon his being in a good humor. . . . Does a man ever speak to his wife and children except to find fault. . . . It is only in books that people fall in love with their wives." Many diaries and letters speak

40. *Race and Nationality in American Life* (Boston: Little, Brown, 1957), p. 148. The whole chapter "The Horrors" is relevant here. Of course, measuring happiness, much less comparing it from one person or period to another, is something no historian has yet found a way to do. Hence the comparative statements sometimes made about the greater degree of happiness in marriage at one period or another are entirely intuitive. It seems likely that the supposedly "disintegrating" family of the twentieth century may represent, on balance, a larger number of comfortable relationships than did the "stable" family of the early nineteenth century, though expectations regarding marriage may have differed from present-day ones. The only thing that can be said with a degree of certainty is that when women had few alternatives to marriage a great deal of discontent was suppressed. See chapter 9 below for Ernest Groves guess about the degree of repression of unhappiness in the nineteenth century.

openly of bitter unhappiness, and one woman prayed to be able to control her "roving fancy." [41]

Such evidence of domestic discontent is reinforced by the observations of southern ministers. A North Carolina Quaker named Thomas Arnett, for example, published a biting critique of family life as it had come under his view. Parents, he said, were capricious in their discipline and preoccupied with false values. John Bayley, a Virginia Methodist, devoted a whole book to the varieties of marital unhappiness he saw around him, and urged both men and women to become more reflective about this vital institution. The practical advice he offered suggests what he had observed: Wives should be neat and clean. ("A minister who travels extensively sees how many wives become disgracefully negligent in a short time. When I have visited some places, and have looked at the wife and children I have soon understood why the husband was seldom at home in his leisure hours.") It was very important to take care of health. ("Every third woman with whom we meet is an invalid.") Husbands should honor their wives, tend the flame of affection, and defeat the whole idea of the "rights of women" by keeping their wives happy.[42]

Augustus Baldwin Longstreet was also a minister—but only incidentally. He was successively president of three colleges, a lawyer of some repute, and best known to poster-

41. *Diary from Dixie;* and also see, for example, Diary of Laura Beecher Comer, SHC UNC; Diary of E. G. C. Thomas, MS Dept., Duke; Diary of Mrs. Isaac Hilliard, Department of Archives, LSU; Mrs. M. E. Jones to Mrs. Mary Burwell, 14 March 1836, Burwell Papers, MS Dept., Duke; Sarah Morgan Diary, MS Dept., Duke; Martha Foster Crawford Diary, October 1849, MS Dept., Duke; Diary of Lucilla McCorkle, January 1852, SHC UNC.

42. *Marriage As It Is,* pp. 113–19.

ity as the author of *Georgia Scenes,* which he offered to the public in 1835 as a reasonably accurate description of life in middle Georgia. One of his stories, "A Charming Creature," offers much the same criticism of marriage, albeit in fictional form. The "charming creature" was a beautiful girl, daughter of a successful businessman in a Georgia town, who had been sent to school in Philadelphia to polish her feminine arts. So successful was she in this endeavor that, when she came home, a hardworking, intelligent young lawyer was completely taken in by her flirtatious ways. After amusing herself for a while, as cat with mouse, she lured him to the altar. Naturally her coquettish habits, so well cultivated, did not disappear after marriage, and her total lack of domestic training led to miserable housekeeping and unbearable extravagance. Her disillusioned husband was driven to drink and an early death. Longstreet's young woman had been raised to believe that the most important thing in her life was her "magic spell"—the ability to entice a man into marriage—but there her education ended. The consequences were disastrous.

If, as the evidence suggests, marriages so eagerly sought were not always satisfactory afterward; if family life for all its potential joys was shadowed by the deaths of children and constant pregnancy; if the lord and master, in close daily encounter, turned out not to be the superior being of the myth; if his sexual freedom was in marked contrast to the perfect chastity of thought and deed demanded of his wife, it was no wonder that some women wondered why life had to be so one-sided. One young woman lamented in her diary: "Oh! the disadvantages we labor under, in not possessing the agreeable independence with the men; tis shameful that all the superiority, authority and freedom in all things should by partial Nature be thrown into their scale."[43] Another, very happily married, occasionally expressed a sense of injustice: ". . . what a drag it is sometimes on a woman to 'lug about' the ladder upon which man plants his foot and ascends to the intellectual heaven of peace in ignorance of the machinery which feeds his daily life."[44] The wife of a distinguished Louisiana judge who would invent a wholly new pattern of life for herself after the war, found housewifely chores a bore and longed for an opportunity to develop her literary and political interests. Guilt-ridden, she looked for religious consolation and made stern resolutions to do better. "I . . . am determined to be more contented . . . in the future."[45]

An anonymous author, probably female, writing in the *Southern Ladies Companion* in 1849 cried out against the paradox of demanding perfection from an inferior being.

Much is always expected of her, in all the spheres of life where she is found. And particularly as a matron, where the functions of wife, mother and mistress are all blended, she is expected to perform duties so complicated and important in character, and so far-reaching in their ultimate consequences, as would require all the tact of the diplomatist, the wisdom of the sage, and the graces of the perfect Christian. In a word, she is expected to be a living encyclopedia of human endowments and perfections. . . .

And yet these very sticklers for perfection . . . on woman's part, are not infrequently found to hold surprising opinions as to her natural inferiority to the other sex. . . . A singular

43. Elizabeth Ruffin, undated diary, SHC UNC.
44. Edmonston, "Diary of Looking Glass Plantation," 2 May 1862.
45. Caroline Merrick to "my dear friend," 18 September 1855 and 27 December 1858, Dept. of Archives, LSU.

phenomenon this, for which a satisfactory explanation would be thankfully received.[46]

There followed an impassioned statement of the injustice of the one-sided emphasis upon education for men, the denial to women of any right to mental cultivation or even of preparation for what all agreed were womanly responsibilities. "The wonder is," said the author caustically, "that women generally make out as well as they do in after life." The article was signed at Charleston.

In view of the definition of woman's role in the South, it is understandable that a southern woman should have written the earliest systematic expression in America of the whole set of ideas constituting the ideology of "woman's rights." Sarah Grimké was born in Charleston in 1792, one of the numerous progeny of a distinguished judge. As a young girl she had expressed the desire to study law. There is no record of her father's response, but he is said to have remarked that if she had been a man she would have become a great jurist. Whether the story is true hardly matters. It sums up the attitude which led Judge Grimké's daughter, and many other able women, to revolt against the social norms.

Early in life Sarah Grimké developed an intense concern about the institution of slavery. In 1821 she struck out on her own for Philadelphia, where she worked with the Friends and took to the platform to denounce slaveholding. When her public speaking was criticized as "unwomanly" she was moved to write *Letters on the Equality of the Sexes.* Published in 1837, these letters constitute a lucid critique of

46. *Southern Ladies Companion,* November 1849, p. 169.

the whole nineteenth-century image of woman, and of the effect it had upon the lives of women—particularly upon women's education, upon what women were led by custom to expect and upon their legal status, and upon women's own choices of the way they spent that most precious commodity, time. No part of the image escaped her devasting pen. She urged women to adopt a new and different ideal of womanhood.

She went at once to what she saw as the heart of the problem: women were "taught to regard marriage as the one thing needful, the only avenue of distinction." From this basic premise a whole train of evils followed. Since men took the initiative in proposing marriage, it was only natural for women to develop those aspects of their personalities they believed to be attractive to men and to suppress the others. Their intellectual development suffered, for men were known to shun intellectual women. Because men demanded it, women had come to regard themselves as no more than "pretty toys" or "mere instruments of pleasure," rather than as whole human beings with souls to be saved and work to do in the world. The premise that marriage was woman's central goal led to the neglect of her education, which meant not only that women failed to develop fully but that children were shortchanged in their education, which in the early years came from their mothers.

Sarah Grimké did not limit her analysis to the effect of the chivalric ideal and the assumption of female inferiority upon her own social class. She was one of the first American social critics to recognize that as women were drawn into employment away from home they were paid much less than their male counterparts and that their belief in their own inferiority, combined with a very poor bargaining position, diminished their capacity to fight back. In every class women's lack of self-respect led to still other consequences:

. . . women being educated, from earliest childhood, to regard themselves as inferior creatures, have not that self-respect which conscious equality would engender, and hence when their virtue is assailed, they yield to temptation with facility, under the idea that it rather exalts than debases them to be connected with a superior being.[47]

She was concerned, too, about slave women whose virtue, she argued, was wholly at the mercy of "irresponsible tyrants."

She tried to show that men would gain by granting the equality of women, since they would find educated women intelligent companions, though she was convinced that, as a rule, men were not anxious to see women improve. She argued that it was ruinous to men and women alike for women to be parasites, and that if women felt the responsibility to support themselves it would add "strength and dignity to their characters." She discussed the question of woman's innate capacity, the problems of dress, of legal disability, and of the relationships of husbands and wives as she had observed them. She also undertook to examine and refute Saint Paul's dictum that women should be silent in the churches.[48]

Sarah Grimké's views on slavery were not unusual, though she and her sister Angelina were among the few open southern abolitionists. As a theorist of male-female relationships, however, she stood alone among southern women for two generations. Sarah Grimké thought she had been badly

47. *Letters on the Equality of the Sexes* (Boston: I. Knapp, 1838), p. 51.
48. Ibid., pp. 47–55.

educated: ". . . the powers of my mind have never been allowed expansion; in childhood they were repressed by the false idea that a girl need not have the education I coveted."[49]

Whatever a better education might have done for her, her *Letters* was based on wide reading and was well reasoned and well written. Like Mary Wollstonecraft and Margaret Fuller, she was a very intelligent woman, intelligent enough to know that she was not an inferior being. Yet intelligence alone does not account for the self-confidence which permitted her to break away from family and home, to encourage her sister to do likewise, and to become a dangerous radical even by northern standards. Something in the Grimkés' early experience had given them an independence of mind uncommon among nineteenth-century women. Their mother, an aristocratic Charleston lady, while deploring the course her daughters had taken, never abandoned them and continued to write affectionate letters as long as she lived.[50]

About the time that Sarah Grimké, from her refuge in the North was attacking the assumptions upon which southern society based its image of woman, one of the South's leading intellectuals was taking issue with these assumptions from another direction. Thomas R. Dew was a professor at William and Mary College; in 1836 he would be its president. He taught an unusual political science course based less on didactic precepts of government than on a study of comparative institutions. He had also applied his fine mind to developing a thoroughgoing justification of slavery. In 1835

49. S. Grimké to Harriot Hunt, 31 December 1852, Weld Papers, William L. Clements Library, University of Michigan.
50. See Lerner, *The Grimké Sisters,* and Barnes and Dumond, *Letters of Theodore Dwight Weld* et al.

he published three articles entitled "The Characteristic Differences between the Sexes." [51] Like his lectures on history and government, his articles were based on comparative analysis. Hastily read, they might be taken for an intolerably long statement of the classic southern position on women. On closer analysis, however, it is clear that Dew did much more than restate what everyone agreed on.

Dew questioned the assumption that the characteristics which the image demanded were God-given. He questioned whether women were *by nature* emotional, naturally inferior and subject to men. He pointed out that education in sex roles began at so early an age that it was impossible to determine "whether their moral and intellectual differences are due wholly to education or partly to nature." He noted also that his analysis applied to everyone of either sex and not to individuals.

. . . for the individual female will frequently be found to have all the masculine traits of character more perfectly developed than the individual man. Few men, for example, can be compared to an Edgeworth or De Stael in point of intellect—and few have shown more persevering courage and masculine heroism, than Queen Margaret of England or Joan d'Arc of France.

Echoing Adam Smith on the influence of occupation on personality, he pointed out that the way women spent their time accounted for much that was considered typically "feminine" in their behavior. The only characteristics of women which he considered to have been given by nature were physical weakness and the capacity for maternity. Both shaped women's typical behavior. Lacking the physi-

51. *Southern Literary Messenger* 1 (1835): 493–512, 621–23, 672–91.

cal prowess to protect themselves or to get what they wanted in the world, they had no recourse save their "magic spell"—hence it was that "grace, modesty and loveliness" had come to be instruments of power. The cultivation of these qualities, which Sarah Grimké found so degrading and the practical results of which Longstreet thought disastrous, Professor Dew found altogether charming. But like Miss Grimké, he thought physical beauty inadequate unless combined with beauty of mind.

Motherhood was obviously a natural function, and he did not fail to note its effect on women's character. Babies took so much time, he suggested, that if a woman were ambitious in law or politics or any profession, she would soon find herself outdistanced by men who were not tied to the nursery and the sickroom. Since few women in Dew's tidewater Virginia circles aspired to law or politics, he was obviously responding to currents from outside. He admitted to having read Mary Wollstonecraft.

Like Sarah Grimké he thought that the emphasis on marriage had shaped the prevailing female character. Since men were expected to do the wooing, they were free to express romantic interests or sexual attraction. Women, who had to wait to be asked, learned early to keep their feelings under cover, sometimes with bad results. A woman who was "frequently required to suppress the most violent feelings; to put a curb on her most ardent desires . . . can suffer much, she can suffer long, in silence without complaint." Feelings which must thus be suppressed, he suggested, might be destroyed.

Dew discussed the opportunities provided by southern culture for men to develop their full potential and observed that women, by contrast, were forced into an unnatural amiability: "The desire to please is undoubtedly the ruling passion of the female heart. . . . Women are precisely what men make them, all over the world." And, he added, "Addison says that had women determined their own point of honor, it is probable that wit or good nature would have carried it against chastity, but our sex have preferred the latter, and woman has conformed to the decision."

In short, Dew liked sweet, gentle, beautiful, shy, modest, domestic women but was under no illusion that God had made them that way. On the contrary, such women were products of a particular culture, a particular kind of conditioning—above all, they followed a particular pattern of male expectation. The image had, to a point, the power to shape reality. It is not clear whether Dew was fully aware of the implications of asking many of the central questions toward which women themselves were groping.

An increasing number of southern men, many of them ministers or college presidents, were beginning to raise some of the same points and some of them went considerably beyond Dew. These men, too, attacked the assumption of female inferiority—at least intellectual inferiority—and advocated a more serious and thorough education for women. Their central themes had appeared at least as early as the eighteenth century when there had been a flurry of concern for educating women "as companions not as playthings for men." The idea had never wholly disappeared from the didactic literature.[52] In practice, however, when marriage at fifteen or sixteen was common, the time allocated for in-

52. See F. . . . L. . . . Esquire, *The Female Friend; or The Duties of Christian Virgins* (Baltimore: H. S. Keatinge, 1809); James M. Garnett, *Seven Lectures on Female Education,* 2d ed. (Richmond: T. W. White, 1824.)

struction was short; and while numerous female seminaries and academies were scattered about the South, not much could be said for the rigors of their curriculums or the qualifications of the teachers.

"I entered at fifteen years and six months and graduated at sharp seventeen," Rebecca Felton remembered. "I took the entire course, also lessons on the piano and guitar." [53] Mrs. Felton and a good many others had the stamina to carry on a lifelong program of self-education. But on the whole, such a hop, step, and jump over a supposedly academic course could not produce lasting effects.

By the 1830s the inadequacy of women's education was a favorite topic for public speakers. The same analysis was repeatedly offered. Dressing their central point in flowery language, a good many men said that women who knew nothing but home skills were often dull and trying wives, not efficient even in dealing with their domestic responsibilities. Since there were no hetaerae in the South's particular version of Greek civilization, a man who wanted to talk to an intelligent woman was confined to his own or someone else's wife.[54] It was desirable, therefore, that wives have something more on their minds than the best recipe for scuppernong wine or the most effective treatment for measles.

A typical exhortation was delivered by the Reverend Mr. W. T. Hamilton of Mobile, speaking at the annual examina-

53. *Country Life in Georgia*, p. 72.
54. Mrs. Chesnut's diary provides material for reflection on this point. Evidently many of the movers and shakers of the Confederacy did enjoy intelligent female companionship, and Mrs. Chesnut was therefore in great demand. She had learned to handle the situation so expertly that her constant association with senators, members of Congress and the cabinet, and military leaders only occasionally led to a domestic uproar.

tion of a female seminary in Marion, Alabama, in 1845. He began with a vigorous plea for "intellectual culture" for women; the mere fact of a narrower sphere of activity, he argued, did not mean that women's minds were less capable of cultivation than those of men and that the only basis for durable respect between the sexes was a cultivated mind. The man who married a well-educated woman was, in Hamilton's view, "blessed beyond ordinary mortals." He denied that intellectual development threatened good housekeeping; it might on the contrary have a beneficial effect. Above all, educated women were more pleasant to have around.[55] An elegant Charleston gentleman, William Porcher Miles, offered much the same argument to the young ladies of the Yorkville Female College, bolstering his case with examples of learned ladies from history.[56]

In 1847 the Reverend William Hooper, president of Wake Forest College, told another female seminary that women needed a solid academic program, with some attention to phyical education. In the background one faintly discerns husbands afflicted by wives with constant headaches. He touched on what may have been the sorest point of all. Shame on man, he said, with all his opportunities for education if he could not keep up with an educated woman. "Woman's rivalry, instead of alarming his jealousy, ought

55. Rev. W. T. Hamilton, *A Plea for the Liberal Education of Women, Delivered at the annual examination of the female seminary under the direction of Rev. S. R. Wright at Marion, Alabama* (New York, 1845), pamphlet in Duke University library.

56. William Porcher Miles, *How to Educate Our Girls, delivered to the young ladies of Yorkville, S.C. Female College* (n.d.), pamphlet in Duke University library. Miles was a lawyer and mathematician who served as mayor of Charleston, a member of Congress, and later a member of the Confederate Congress.

only to let him know the necessity of continued progress, lest she overtake or outstrip him." [57]

Turning the ancient argument about woman's beneficent influence upon men in a new direction, Hooper asserted: "Give us girls as can understand and delight in such a work as *Paradise Lost*, more than in trashy novels or the trashy, insipid chat of town gossip, and I will soon show you a new race of *men*, ambitious to merit and to win the noble hearts of such a race of women." [58] And, throwing light upon the domestic scene: "Shall the beautiful half of creation be just like a collection of pictures and statues, pleasing the eye but having no graces of mind to match these external graces . . . [and] as soon as she opens her mouth shall enchantment vanish by the utterance of coarse and vulgar ideas, and of low, ungrammatical language?" [59]

Urging fathers to worry less about saving money for a dowry and more about spending it wisely to educate their daughters, Hooper pointed out that with the inevitable fading of youth and beauty a woman needed other resources. And since women were so often the center of a family's religious life, religion itself was denigrated when they were ignorant. Finally, husbands could not respect ignorant

57. Rev. William Hooper, *Address on Female Education, delivered before the Sedgewick Female Seminary, Feb. 27, 1847,* pamphlet in Duke University library. The hazards to which the good reverend adverted—if a woman were too well educated the men might have trouble keeping up —are amusingly documented in the diary of Joseph LeConte's young daughter Emma, who had been reading Hitchcock's *Religion and Geology:* "I find a good many ideas there that M. in our talks advanced as his own—sometimes expressed in the identical words. I think he had recently read the book!" Diary of Emma LeConte, 5 February 1865, SHC UNC.
58. Hooper, *Address on Female Education*, p. 23.
59. Ibid., p. 9.

wives; and a mother who did not have the respect of the father would be looked down on by her children.

Repeated variations on this argument appeared, in periodicals, journals, speeches, and sermons. In their own way, in short, respected southern gentlemen echoed Sarah Grimké's demand for female education. But if they denied the intellectual inferiority of women, they upheld most of the other elements of the mythical southern lady. None of them suggested any real expansion in woman's "sphere." Their point was that an educated woman could inhabit the sphere more gracefully and conduct her female responsibilities more effectively.[60]

All the male arguments for improving female education were founded upon two or three premises: that women had undeveloped intellectual capacities, that educated women made better wives and better mothers (and hence a better society), and that educated women were better companions.

60. See Richard Gladney, *Essays on Female Education* (Columbia, S.C., 1832); William Carey Richards in *The Orion* 2 (December 1842): 120–23; *Southern Literary Messenger* 1 (May 1835): 519; 5 (September 1839): 597–601; President George Foster Pierce, Baccalureate Address, 18 July 1840, reprinted in *Wesleyan Alumni Review*, May 1940; William H. Felton, *Address Delivered at the Annual Commencement of the Madison Female College, 1853*, pamphlet in Duke University library; *Southern Ladies Companion*, 1848–49, pp. 133–34; *North Carolina Journal of Education*, July 1859; Elias Marks, M.D., of Barhamville, S.C., *Hints on Female Education* (Columbia, S.C., 1851); Rev. Joseph R. Wilson, D.D., *Female Training, a Sermon Delivered before the Friends of the Greensboro Female College, May 23, 1858, August, 1858,* pamphlet in Duke University library. In view of all this discussion it is not surprising to find the years 1830–60 fertile in the founding of new colleges, seminaries, and academies for women. Many were ephemeral but a few struck deeper roots and made a serious effort. Some of these, as Wesleyan College at Macon, Georgia, and Greensboro College in North Carolina still exist. See I. M. E. Blandin, *History of Higher Education of Women in the South prior to 1860* (New York: Neal Publishing Co., 1909).

These gentlemen did not consider the possible consequences of their advice. Southern men who assented to laws forbidding slaves to be taught to read and write should have understood that it was risky to educate anyone whom they wished to keep in a degree of subjection. If enough women had an opportunity for the significant intellectual development they were advocating, would they then be satisfied to remain in the sphere into which men and society cast them?

An interesting example of what might happen occurred in Chapel Hill. Two members of the University of North Carolina faculty, Elisha Mitchell and James Phillips, decided in the 1840s to give their daughters an education equal to that of the young men in the college. The Mitchell girls and Cornelia Phillips were tutored by their fathers, attended college classes, and were encouraged to read and study systematically. All three were bright, and at least one undergraduate thought Cornelia Phillips "the smartest girl I know" and added that if *only* she had had money he would certainly have courted her! [61]

What was the result? Hope Summerell Chamberlain, Ellen Mitchell's daughter, thought her mother had been made forever discontented with the ordinary round of women's activity.

Restless my mother was, with active mind and ever-skillful hands. The sense of restraint and inefficacy, the desire to use some of her abundant vitality beyond the bounds of her environment, made her thoughts widely wandering. . . .
Too much mental activity in a woman is still considered a nuisance. In those old days, learning might still be pardoned in a man, but it was a monstrous excrecence [*sic*] upon a wom-

61. Sanders, ed., "The Diary of Ruffin Wirt Tomlinson," p. 254.

anly personality. Accordingly, neither then or later did Mother talk much of her mental excursions.[62]

As for Cornelia Phillips, the effects of her unusual education reached into the twentieth century, as will presently appear. For the moment it is necessary only to observe an entry in her diary, made shortly after the Civil War:

> But I feel sometimes such an impatience of my life and its narrow lot as I can scarcely describe. I want to go and see something better than I have ever known. . . . I want to go, to take wings and fly and leave these sordid occupations. . . .
> I think sometimes it is cruel to cultivate tastes that are never to be gratified in this world.[63]

For many women, the desire for education beyond that accorded them was a source of discontent. Rarely doubting their own mental capacities, they complained bitterly about the absence of educational opportunities. A fifteen-year-old girl in Louisiana, for example:

> I wish to go to studying again for I feel more than ever before my great ignorance in all that pertains to knowledge. . . . I know nothing of the sciences and no language except my own and a little of the latin, and then there are accomplishments.[64]

Two years later the same girl recorded in one month's diary entries that she was reading Prescott's *Conquest of Mexico,* Humboldt's *Cosmos,* and Milton's *Paradise Lost.*

A young matron in eastern Georgia, mother of several children, noted in her Journal in 1857:

62. Hope Chamberlain, *This Was Home,* pp. 85–87.
63. Quoted in ibid., p. 93.
64. Sarah Wadley Diary, 18 October 1860, SHC UNC.

I have been reading Macaulay's Essays—find them both
entertaining and instructive, and wish that I had history at my
tongue's end as he has—I look back at the past ten years of my
life with much regret, for I feel that I have not devoted this
time to intellectual culture as I should have. My mind has I
fear shrunk instead of expanding, but I am going to do better
for myself. I must and will devote more time to study. Oh that
I could lend some aid to lift the cloud which obscures our
Southern intellectual sky.[65]

Elsewhere in Georgia a younger and more frivolous lady
shared some of the same feelings and announced her resolution to resume the study of Latin under the inspiration of
Augusta Evans's *St. Elmo*.[66] A Louisiana girl was startled
into a new view by a long talk with a visiting Confederate
colonel, who told her that she, too, could reason and that the
ignorance she deplored in herself was not inevitable.

And when I . . . looked in my own heart and saw my
shocking ignorance and pitiful inferiority so painfully evident
to my own eyes I actually cried. Why was I denied the
education that would enable me to be the equal of such a
man? [67]

In 1859 a North Carolina woman was emboldened to raise
her voice in public—or, rather, to raise someone else's voice,
since, being female, she was not permitted to read her own
paper to the North Carolina Education Association. Beginning with a lament for "this long neglected topic" and

65. Susan Cornwall Shewmake Journal, 1 May 1857, SHC UNC.
66. Anna Maria Green, *The Journal of a Milledgeville Girl, 1861–67,*
ed. James C. Bonner (Athens, Ga.: University of Georgia Press, 1964).
67. Sarah Morgan Dawson, *A Confederate Girl's Diary* (Boston:
Houghton Mifflin, 1913), pp. 249–50.

apparently unaware of the sympathy she might have found among some men in her region, Delia W. Jones asserted that

> Among our Lords and Masters, no champion can be found ready to fight the battles of ambitious womanhood against folly and ignorance . . . [hence] ourselves should occasionally venture to take up the gauntlet, and in defiance of custom, tell the world that in addition to our known and confessed ability to *talk,* we would also like to *think,* and be taught how to direct thought so as to *talk* more wisely.[68]

As many of these quotations suggest, reading was one of the ways in which women could compensate for their limited intellectual opportunities. Many women read constantly, and while the outcry against novel-reading suggests that much of their reading was for escape and amusement, they also devoted a great deal of time to serious, sometimes naive, efforts to remedy by self-education the deficiencies of formal instruction. Mill's *Political Economy,* Dickens's novels, Madame de Staël's *Corinne,* Bulwer's novels, Plutarch, Boswell, Tennyson, Milton, Huxley, Darwin, were only a few of the authors and titles which sprinkled diary pages. A careful study of one plantation lady's reading habits showed her to be familiar with a wide range of ancient and modern literature, especially Shakespeare, Milton, and the Bible. During the Civil War she became a student of military strategy. There is nothing in her life or background to suggest that she was unique.[69]

Beyond reading there was writing. Helen Papashvily

68. "Manner of Educating Females," *North Carolina Journal of Education,* August 1859.

69. James M. Patton, "Serious Reading in Halifax County, 1860–1865," *North Carolina Historical Review* 42 (April 1965): 169–79.

makes an amusing and persuasive case for the sentimental novel as the weapon with which nineteenth-century women took their revenge upon men.[70] A good number of the novels she discusses were written by southern women. At least two of these, Caroline Lee Hentz and Augusta Evans Wilson, were clear examples of women of more than ordinary talent and energy who found the role of the southern lady restrictive. Mrs. Hentz joined her husband in schoolteaching but found adolescent girls a trial, and in her novels she revealed a good deal of her dissatisfaction with a woman's life.[71] Augusta Evans became not only a best-selling author but a kind of folk heroine in Mobile, where, having married a man old enough to be her father, she presided over a stately mansion. Literary success released her from many of the restrictions customarily laid upon her sex, but she was vehemently opposed to such an escape for other women.

God, the maker, tenderly anchored womanhood in the peaceful blessed haven of home; and if man is ever insane enough to mar the divine economy by setting women afloat on the turbulent roaring sea of politics, they will speedily become pitiable wrecks. . . . Surely utter ignorance is infinitely preferable to erudite unwomanliness.[72]

Mrs. Wilson, who wrote long letters of advice to Congressman J. L. M. Curry and studied history, languages, and philosophy, was not the last woman to achieve an enviable emancipation herself while denying that it was appropriate for others. She had a low opinion of her contemporaries.

70. Helen Waite Papashvily, *All the Happy Endings* (New York: Harper & Bros., 1956).

71. See also Caroline Lee Hentz Diary, passim, SHC UNC.

72. Quoted in William Perry Fidler, *Augusta Evans Wilson* (University, Ala.: University of Alabama Press, 1951), p. 141.

"Southern women are often pleasant and graceful," she wrote in a letter to Curry, but their "information is painfully scanty, their judgement defective, their reasoning faculties dwarfed, their aspirations weak and frivolous." [73]

If deep-seated resentment against the narrowness of educational opportunity and the assumption of intellectual inferiority occasionally broke into the open, resentment against economic dependency was more likely to be kept hidden in the recesses of private diaries. Mrs. Chesnut noted that she had inherited her share of her father's estate soon after her marriage and that it went for debts her husband had already contracted.

That being the case, why feel like a beggar, utterly humiliated and degraded when I am forced to say I need money? I cannot tell, but I do; and the worst of it is, this thing grows worse as one grows older. Money ought not to be asked for, or given to a man's wife as a gift. Something must be due her, and that she should have, and no growling and grumbling nor warnings against waste and extravagance, nor hints as to the need of economy, nor amazement that the last supply has given out already. What a proud woman suffers under all this, who can tell? [74]

"I told him I thought he was extravagant to hire a gardener," wrote a Mississippi woman, "and he seemed hurt —well he might be, for I have no right to say a word, he earns the money. . . . *I* make nothing and have no right to anything but to receive thankfully what is given me." [75]

73. Augusta Evans Wilson to J. L. M. Curry, 15 July 1863, J. L. M. Curry Papers, Manuscripts Division, Library of Congress. See also her *St. Elmo* (New York: Grossett & Dunlap, 1896), pp. 404, 453–54, 482.
74. *Diary from Dixie,* p. 186, 24 January 1862.
75. Diary of Mahala P. Roach, 21 May 1859, SHC UNC.

Other women tried various devices for earning a little money for themselves, though even that, under the law, belonged to their husbands. Selling surplus garden products, giving music lessons, and even writing poems for newspapers were not uncommon.

By the eve of the Civil War a psychological Geiger counter would have detected growing discontent with woman's assigned role.[76] Outside influences contributed to the increasing restiveness of southern women. The 1850s were for the whole United States a decade of economic development, population growth, and considerable population movement. It was also a decade of great political tension and mounting paranoia on the subject of slavery, a period of instability which increased anxiety and fear for the future.

76. One literary historian foreshadowed the thesis of this book in 1925 when he wrote: "The tradition did not so much unreasonably glorify the plantation woman as remain strangely silent about certain important, exceedingly important, phases of her existence. To apprehend dimly the vast unsaid, one need only imagine what a strictly realistic attitude might have made of the material. The tradition does not suggest, as a matter of fact, the status of women under the slavery regime. Honored with a real, a peculiar reverence, the boast and the idol of masculine society, she was, nevertheless, the pathetic victim of that society. The pleasant legend does not develop the excessive chaperonage which hedged her in, the denial of development which we recognize as hers by right, the utter economic dependence of these high-spirited women. Particularly notable is the failure of the tradition to hint at a certain orientalism which operated from the moment when the belle, abdicating her throne of social dominion, yielded herself to the program of the plantation lord. This 'till death do us part' theory had under the conditions of the old regime, a tremendous literalness fraught with terrible possibilities. In all romance there is a conspicuous absence of the psychology of lovely young girls who married young sports and found that matrimony locked a door and threw away the key, locked a door so thick that not even a cry of pain could ever penetrate to the outer world." Francis Pendleton Gaines, *The Southern Plantation* (New York: Columbia University Press, 1925), p. 180.

Even some well-protected southern women heard the rever-
berations which followed the Seneca Falls convention of
1848 and its "Declaration of Sentiments." Where all this
would have led in the absence of a war no one can guess.
But the war came and as wars do, it speeded social change
and opened Pandora's box.

That you and Ida are quite
able to take care of yourselves
I entertain no doubt, but still
it does me good to find you
asserting the fact with so much
boldness. Of all the principles
developed by the late war, I
think the capability of our
Southern women to take care of
themselves was by no means the
least important.

Thomas Dabney to his
daughter Emmy, 13 August
1879, quoted in *Memorials of a
Southern Planter*

4

The War

The Civil War passed over the South like a giant tidal wave, cracking many structures so fatally that it was only a matter of time before they fell to pieces. Some parts of the old order were fitted into the new, which began to emerge even before the war was over; others disappeared entirely.

The breaking up and remaking of institutions affected the whole society and had profound consequences for the lives of southern women. Individuals as well as institutions were altered by the war experience and, like the institutions, some never recovered, while others adapted themselves to the new patterns of the postwar years as best they could.

The visible and immediate consequences of the outbreak of war upon women's lives have been described again and again. The challenge of war called women almost at once into new kinds and new degrees of activity. "They became planters, millers, merchants, manufacturers, managers," wrote one woman.[1] Soldiers' aid societies sprang into being as if southern women had all their lives been used to community organization. The number of these societies approached a thousand, and though some bowed to convention and asked a male clergyman to preside over their meetings, the groups were the result of women's initiative and ran on women's energies.

The North's advantage in manpower was clear from the beginning. In the South the women, left at home without their men, assumed responsibility for maintaining and if possible increasing the food supply, for producing cotton and wool and making clothing, flags, tents, bandages, and other things soldiers needed. This was not purely an administrative effort: women whose closest association with a needle

1. Sally Elmore Taylor, Memoirs, p. 107, SHC UNC.

had been to supervise slave seamstresses were soon prick-
ing their fingers along with their poorer neighbors who were
not so new to the task. The experience of years of providing
food and clothing for slaves was now applied to feeding and
clothing an army.

Husbands hurrying off to the army or to the Confederate
Congress sent back all kinds of instructions about the
planting, harvesting, and marketing of crops, the management of slaves, the education of children, the budgeting of
money, the collecting of old debts, and every other aspect of
their business, apparently in perfect confidence that their
wives would somehow cope. The women, in their turn, were
polite about asking advice and begged for guidance, while
carrying on as if they had always been planters, business
managers, overseers of slaves, and decision makers. Many
would later be confronted with invading soldiers and would
hastily improvise ways to meet that crisis.

The demands of the war cut across class lines. While a
yeoman farmer's wife shouldered burdens of plowing, planting, fence-repairing, and so on, beyond anything expected of
her in peacetime, an aristocratic lady was proud that she
had learned to calculate lumber measurements well enough
to run a sawmill on the Congaree River. War widows and
women whose sources of income had been cut off by the war
became clerks in government offices. Mills, especially those
created to produce supplies for the war, hired women opera-
tors. Schoolteaching was taken over by women, as native
schoolmasters answered the call to arms and those from the
North went home. And, *in extremis,* almost any woman
could sew for money.

A return to handweaving and spinning was noted all over
the South. Mrs. Clay remembered that "old spinning wheels

and handlooms were brought out from dusty corners, and the whirr of the wheel became a very song to us. Every scrap of old leather from furniture, trunk, belt or saddle was saved for the manufacture of rough shoes, often made by the mother who had been fortunate enough to have hoarded them for herself and children." [2]

With the first battle, the care of sick and wounded men became a central focus of women's concern. The least demanding form of service was that of sending supplies, and for this purpose hospital aid societies were organized in many communities. Women with a greater urge to make sacrifices could nurse, as many did, and the sturdiest souls became hospital matrons or superintendents, often to the dismay of male surgeons.

Louisa Cheves McCord, eldest daughter of Langdon Cheves, organized a soldier's hospital in Columbia, South Carolina, taking over buildings on the college campus for the purpose. "Mrs. McCord is as little afraid of personal responsibility as the Jacksons, Andrew or Stonewall," commented her friend Mary Chesnut. When the McCords' only son, not yet twenty-one, died from battle wounds, Mrs. Chesnut added, "She is dedicating her grief for her son . . . by giving up her soul and body, her days and nights, to the wounded soldiers." [3]

Phoebe Yates Pember, member of a large and distinguished Savannah family, became head matron of a hospital in Richmond. Her arrival did not delight the chief surgeon, who shared the suspicion of many of his brethren that the advent of women was bound to lead to an unpleasant form of "petticoat government." His fears were gradually allayed

2. *A Belle of the Fifties* (New York, 1905), p. 223.
3. *Diary from Dixie*, pp. 243, 425.

by experience, and for four years Mrs. Pember carried on every imaginable sort of labor while organizing and administering the hospital in the interests of better care for the wounded and more efficiency in the use of medical resources. She even took charge of the whiskey barrel, one aspect of the hospital the misuse of which was causing her great trouble. And, when a group of drunken soldiers entered her apartment in search of the precious supply of whiskey, she held them at bay with a pistol. Her diary, a running account of her experiences in the hospital, reveals a tough, hard-working administrator who preserved her sanity with a fine sense of humor.[4] She had nothing but scorn for the notion that no southern lady would be found in such a rude circumstance as an army hospital:

> There is one subject connected with hospitals on which a few words must be said—the distasteful one that a woman must lose a certain amount of delicacy and reticence in filling any office in them. How can this be? . . . the circumstances which surround a wounded man, far from friends and home, suffering in a holy cause and dependent upon a woman for help, care and sympathy, hallow and clear the atmosphere in which she labors. . . . In the midst of suffering and death, hoping with those almost beyond hope in this world, praying by the bedside of the lonely and heart-stricken; closing the eyes of boys hardly old enough to realise man's sorrows, much less suffer by man's fierce hate, a woman must soar beyond the conventional modesty considered correct under different circumstances.[5]

Kate Cumming of Mobile was born in Scotland, but grew up a southern lady. She responded to a minister's appeal for ladies to go to the front and nurse the wounded, though her family disapproved and she herself admitted, "I had never

4. Phoebe Yates Pember, *A Southern Woman's Story* (New York: G. W. Carleton, 1879).
5. *A Southern Woman's Story*, p. 192.

been inside of a hospital and was wholly ignorant of what I should be called upon to do, but I knew that what one woman [Florence Nightingale] had done another could." [6] Most of her fellow volunteers from Mobile (including the novelist Augusta Evans) changed their minds, but she persisted, was put in charge of a hospital, and by 1862 was regularly enlisted in the Confederate medical department. Like Mrs. Pember, Kate Cumming was a strong woman with a considerable capacity for administration, and though she lacked Mrs. Pember's sense of humor she shared her fortitude in facing the endless arrival of sick and wounded soldiers for whom so little could be done. She shared, also, an astonishing capacity to endure physical hardship, evidence for which appears on almost every page of her diary. Perhaps her own patient courage lay behind her scorn for those less tough than herself. "A young lady, . . . one of the handsomest women in Mobile, sat near me at table, and when I told her how I had been employed since the war, she said she had often wished to do the same. I wondered what ʾhindered her." [7]

Sally Louisa Tompkins, a twenty-eight-year-old spinster in Richmond, commandeered a friend's house and made it into a hospital whose life-saving record was so impressive that in order to assure the continuation of her work, the Confederate government made her a captain in the army. She was said to have treated, during the whole war, more than 1,300 soldiers and to have lost only 73. [8] Ella King

6. Kate Cumming, *Gleanings from the Southland* (Birmingham, Ala.: Roberts & Son, 1895), pp. 37–38.

7. *Kate: The Journal of a Confederate Nurse,* ed. Richard Barksdale Harwell (Baton Rouge: Louisiana State University Press, 1959), p. 244.

8. "Sally Louisa Tompkins," sketch in the *Dictionary of American Biography*. See also Matthew Page Andrews, *The Women of the South in War Times* (Baltimore: Norman Remington, 1920), passim.

Newsome, a wealthy Arkansas widow, used her own money as well as her time and energy in a series of hospitals which moved ahead of the Yankees; she came, inevitably, to be called "the Florence Nightingale of the South." Mrs. Newsome's skill was apparently equaled by her charm and tact, so that her example considerably diminished the social disapproval visited upon women who worked in hospitals.

For many women life after 1862 was a series of traumas. As they worked to keep plantations, farms, and homes going, the fate of husbands and sons in the army was a constant source of anxiety. One old soldier, reminiscing in the eighties, thought it had been harder for the women than for the soldiers themselves: the soldier at least knew if he was still alive, while his wife worried constantly. Many familes had several sons in uniform; one was recorded with twelve sons in combat, nine of whom were killed. Josephine Habersham's boys survived one battle after another only to die together very near the end of the war. Hetty Cary, said to be the most beautiful girl in Richmond, married her soldier sweetheart and returned to the same church two weeks later for his funeral. A South Carolina woman lost five brothers and a fiancé before the carnage ended.[9] Toward the end of the war an Atlanta woman wrote:

Were these the same people—these haggard, wrinkled women, bowed with care and trouble, sorrow and unusual toil? These tame, pale, tearless girls, from whose soft flesh the witching dimples had long since departed, or were drawn down into furrows—were they the same school girls of 1861? These women who, with coarse, lean and brown hands . . . these women with scant, faded cotton gowns and coarse leather shoes

9. E. Merton Coulter, *Lost Generation* (Tuscaloosa: University of Alabama Press, 1956), p. 101.

—these women who silently and apathetically packed the boxes, looking into them with the intense and sorrowful gaze that one casts into the tomb.[10]

Then there were the invasions of northern armies, especially Sherman's. Not only was it Sherman's fixed policy to destroy so much that the people in his path would lose their taste for war entirely but many units of his army were simply out of control, running wild in their urge to harass and destroy. The widow and daughter of a wealthy minister-planter of Liberty County, Georgia, were visited by successive groups of soldiers from Sherman's army late in 1864, each group repeating the search and seizure of its predecessor. Neither the white hairs of the mother nor the pregnancy of the daughter protected them against the soldiers' wanton cruelty, such as the theft of the only remaining well chain, so that the women could no longer draw water.[11]

The experiences, and reactions, of southern women were similar in broad outline but varied enormously in detail.

The broadest division was simply between those who faced up to the demands of the times and those who evaded them or ran away. In some parts of the South, where the invader never came, it was possible for the first two years to go on living a fairly normal life. This was especially true for young women who were not yet betrothed and who had no

10. Quoted in Francis W. Dawson, "Our Women in the War," delivered 22 February 1887 to the Fifth Annual Reunion of the Association of the Maryland Line.

11. Mary Sharpe Jones and Mary Jones Mallard, *Yankees a'Coming,* ed. Haskell Monroe (Tuscaloosa: University of Alabama Press, 1950). This is a diary kept day by day during the invasion. Vol. 2 of Grace Elmore's diary, typescript in the SHC UNC, is an equally graphic contemporary report of the activities of Sherman's men in Columbia, South Carolina.

father or brother in the service. By the end of the war the number who fitted this description must have been small. Other women, with men in the army and challenges all around them, tried to continue a gay social life, and though some succeeded for a time this response, too, became more difficult to maintain as the years passed. A few actually ran away, to Canada or to Europe, to evade entirely, in Justice Holmes's phrase, the action and passion of their times.

Among those who tried to face rather than to escape the conditions created by the war, differences in response were a function of age, health, energy, intelligence, disposition, and circumstance. Some were called to bear more than others, and it is not surprising that older women, losing a husband or several sons, seeing all their material possessions go up in smoke or disappear into Yankee pockets, would sometimes simply give up and die, or become so broken in spirit that death came prematurely not long after the war was over.

Some women who rose to the needs of the times were frank about their distaste for the enterprise. A South Carolina woman wrote to her husband in the Confederate Congress:

Several pigs have died. . . . I tell [you] candidly all this attention to farming is uphill work with me. I can give orders first-rate, but when I am not obeyed, I can't keep my temper. A housekeeper has so much to do independent of field work. Then our [soldiers' aid] society keeps us busy. I am ever ready to give you a helping hand, but I must say I am heartily tired of trying to manage free negroes. . . . it is so lonesome here.[12]

Another husband in the Confederate Congress asked his wife for more information:

12. Mrs. W. W. Boyce to her husband 12 April 1862, MS in private hands, quoted in Bell I. Wiley, ed., *Letters of Warren Akin* (Athens, Ga:, University of Georgia Press, 1959), pp. 5–6.

Your letters are *very* short. Why don't you write more? . . .
Tell me everything that is done, what the little children say
and do, how the stable and the crib are furnished—whether my
mules and corn etc. are safe in them, how the mules look, how
much milk the cows give, how often you churn, how the wheat
looks . . . do the boys study? [13]

The poor woman tried harder, and wrote longer letters, but
obliquely suggested that one reason for the shortness of her
communications was the length of her list of obligations.
She not only had the plantation and the children to manage,
but she was a refugee from home, farming on land not her
own; she was constantly beset with creditors and was having trouble collecting money owed to her husband. She rose
at dawn, she said, and fell into bed at nine, not to sleep but
to toss and turn as she worried about her responsibilities.
Her letters nevertheless were full of affection, and the desire
to please him. Although she was only thirty-four to his
fifty-three she responded to his statement that he felt strong
and young by saying:

I am truly glad to know you have such good health and feel
strong and *young*. I have excellent health and I don't feel
young at all, and I'm sure I look old, my hair will soon be
white. It is very gray now and gets more so every week.[14]

Plantation wives and mothers had a straightforward, if
demanding, path laid before them. A city-dwelling spinster
might have more difficulty knowing how to respond to the
war. One wrote:

In the meantime we are leading the lives which women have
led since Troy fell; wearing away time with memories, re-
grets and fears; alternating fits of suppression, with flights,

13. Warren Akin to his wife 11 December 1864, ibid., p. 37.
14. Ibid., p. 119.

imaginary, to the red fields . . . while men, more privi-
leged . . . make name and fortune while helping to make a
nation. . . . I am like a pent-up volcano. I wish I had a field
for my energies.[15]

Still another style of life fell upon many women who had
to leave their homes and live as refugees, moving from place
to place, often keeping their children and themselves alive
only by exercising immense ingenuity and courage.[16]

However courageously a woman might meet her particular version of the crisis, there were points beyond which
some could not go. The files of Governor Zebulon Vance of
North Carolina were filled with pitiful, sometimes self-pity-
ing, letters from women who felt they could go on no longer
and wanted their husbands mustered out before the family
starved to death.[17]

It took a little while for anyone to realize that southern
women were experiencing what was for many of them a new
condition : life without a man around to make decisions. It
was 1865, perhaps, before the realization struck home—for
the condition had seemed temporary and many people were
too busy to be very reflective. After four years of war a
South Carolina woman observed :

How queer the times, the women can't count on the men
at all to help them; they either laugh at us or when they

15. *Journal of Julia LeGrand,* ed. Kate Mason Rowland and Mrs.
Morris Croxall (Richmond: Everett Waddey, 1911), p. 52.

16. A good example is found in the life of Elizabeth Avery Meriwether, described in her *Recollections of 92 Years* (Nashville: Tennessee
Historical Commission, 1958) ; others in Mrs. Clay's *Belle of the Fifties,*
cited in n. 2 above, and in Judith McGuire, *Diary of a Southern Refugee*
(New York: E. J. Hale & Son, 1867).

17. Francis B. Simkins and James W. Patton, *The Women of the
Confederacy* (Richmond and New York: Garrett & Massie, 1936), p.
226.

speak seriously it is to say they know not what to advise, we must do the best of our ability. . . . Our men depend on us a great deal, in fact their time and thought are so fully occupied with what concerns the public welfare that they have none to spare for private matters.[18]

The end of the war did not improve conditions for southern women. "The war was prosperity to the state of things which peace has wrought," one woman wrote.

The women in every community seemed to far outnumber the men; and the empty sleeve and the crutch made men who had unflinchingly faced death in battle impotent to face their future. Sadder still was it to follow to the grave the army of men, of fifty years and over when the war began, whose hearts broke with the loss of half a century's accumulations and ambitions, and with the failure of the cause for which they had risked everything. Communities were accustomed to lean upon these tried advisers; it was almost like the slaughter of another army—so many sank beneath the shocks of reconstruction. . . . So in these days of awful uncertainties when men's hearts failed them, it was the woman who brought her greater adaptabliity and elasticity to control circumstances, and to lay the foundations of a new order.[19]

Like the older men, many younger ones who had survived the fighting were mustered out broken in body and spirit. The homes they came back to were hardly recognizable, for even in the large areas which had never heard the tramp of marching feet, the blockade and the demands of the war for material wealth had done their damage. With the psychological goad of a patriotic war at an end, it was still necessary

18. Grace Elmore Diary, 11 February 1865, Columbia, S.C., typescript, vol. 2, SHC UNC.
19. Caroline Merrick, *Old Times in Dixie Land* (New York, 1901), pp. 75–76.

to make do in a thousand ways simply to provide a minimum of food and clothing. And the freedmen were wandering about, freedom meaning, in its first interpretation, freedom to leave the accustomed plantation. There was no
experience to guide people in so total a disaster, greater than
any previous disruption by epidemic or economic depression
or natural calamity.

Such was life in the South, varying from time to time and
place to place, for a decade after the war ended. Of the
million men who at one time or another had served in the
Confederate army one-fourth, at least, had died from
wounds or disease, and no one knows how many others were
crippled or debilitated for life. Many parts of the South had
been devastated by northern armies; towns like Columbia
and Richmond had been burned; Sherman had left Atlanta
in ashes; Charleston had been repeatedly bombarded and
had suffered from two large fires. Transportation was destroyed. Neither the freedmen nor their former masters had
a clear idea of how they were to be fitted into the postwar
society and economy. Even if there had been no labor problem, the materials the farmers needed to get back to work
were lacking: livestock, machinery, and seed.

In Alabama alone there were eighty thousand widows,
three-fourths of whom were said to be in want of the bare
necessities of life. Sidney Lanier's often quoted plaint:
"Perhaps you know that with us of the young generation in
the South, since the war, pretty much the whole of life has
been merely not dying," may be taken to cover very many
people who had grown up in the late fifties and lost five
years of their late youth to the war itself. Pride of class had
to be put aside. A Charleston woman noted that "Henry
Manigault and his wife are Steward & Matron of the Alms

House in Charleston, Williams Middleton is renting out his rooms; James Hayward's wife and daughters . . . are taking in sewing; Mrs. Allston, the Gov's widow keeps a boarding house." [20] The writer's own daughter had gone out to teach school and when her family, their fortunes mending a bit, ordered her home she announced firmly that independence was to be preferred to a dependent respectability.

"In nothing has the singularity of the times struck me more," wrote Grace Elmore, "than the perfect fortitude with which my people met their fate. . . . Had we time to think ours would be a 'melancholy people.' But now our vocation is work, and we all recognize it to be so, for young and old, men and women, are pushed by a necessity, before unknown, the need of bread. . . . I knew my old life was done." [21] A Virginia matron meditated, "I little thought this time twenty-one years ago when I was putting on my white satin slippers that I should ever cook a dinner for myself, and now I do it every day, & am as happy in these new circumstances as ever before." [22]

Rebecca Latimer Felton, whose two children had died while Sherman was ravaging her plantation in middle Georgia, looked around with her husband to find some means of starting over, and in January 1866 they opened a school.[23] "The women, the courageous women, everywhere were busy reorganizing lives building up new homes out of the wrecks," wrote an Alabama observer.[24]

20. M. M. Grimball Diary, December 1866, SHC UNC.

21. Diary, 21 September 1865.

22. Susannah Gordon Waddell Diary, 7 August 1865, typescript, SHC UNC.

23. John Talmadge, *Rebecca Latimer Felton* (Athens, Ga.: University of Georgia Press, 1960), p. 25.

24. Recollections of Clare C. Raymond, typescript, Part II, SHC UNC.

There was, of course, no single response to the consequences of defeat and surrender. In some ways the South in 1865 became again a frontier where there were few precedents to help people deal with their problems and few supporting structures for those who needed support. Some men showed remarkable resiliency in meeting this challenge, one which (unlike the frontiersman) they had not consciously chosen. As early as August 1865 Cornelia Spencer noted in her diary that her friend Kemp Battle, later to be president of the University of North Carolina, was writing from New York, "taking a strong ground in favor of a hearty reunion with the northern people, inviting and assisting immigration, calling in capital, welcoming workers, opening up every source of national prosperity, and turning over a new leaf generally." [25] Robert R. Cotten, an impecunious Confederate veteran, traveled to New York wearing his uniform for lack of other garb and came home with credit to open a store in Tarboro, North Carolina, which eventually would yield enough profit to enable him to buy the plantation his heart was set upon.[26] Some planters, like the McCollams in Louisiana, went to work at once to restore their damaged plantations, and with considerable success.[27] The South Carolina botanist Henry Ravenel had

25. Hope Summerell Chamberlain, *Old Days in Chapel Hill* (Chapel Hill: University of North Carolina Press, 1926), p. 116.
26. Sallie Southall Cotten Papers, Biographical Notes, June 1916, SHC UNC.
27. J. Carlyle Sitterson, "The McCollams: A Planter Family of the Old and New South," *Journal of Southern History* 6 (August 1940): 347–67; J. L. M. Curry, late of the Confederate Congress, returned to Talledega, Alabama, to find his wife dead and his plantation about to be confiscated. However, the local Baptist college at once made him president, and before 1867 he had sufficiently restored his fortunes to take his second wife honeymooning in Europe. Edwin A. Alderman and Armistead L. Gordon, *J. L. M. Curry* (New York: Macmillan, 1911), pp. 195–206.

patriotically invested his fortune in Confederate bonds and was now reduced to what he could earn selling wood and vegetables from his plantation; yet he noted in his diary that he was as contented poor as he had been rich.[28] Few planters evinced such resignation. More typical was an outcry in the *Southern Cultivator*:

$50 Reward

Is offered for information that will enable me to make a living and make the ends meet on my farm by the use of Negro labor. I have a good farm and all the necessary appliances and have been trying to do the above uphill task for three mortal years of freedom but haven't done it—and have exhausted all my theories and those of my neighbors, and am about giving up the matter for good.[29]

Enterprising though some men were, in looking ahead and adjusting quickly to the needs of a chaotic time and the coming of a new order, to others the demands seemed too great. Clement C. Clay, whose position in the Confederate hierarchy had entitled him to be imprisoned along with Jefferson Davis, came back to Alabama but in spite of heroic efforts was never able to get out of debt. His brothers were not much more successful. Many of the leading members of the old order simply gave up and died, as Mrs. Merrick reported. Others lived on, but never again enjoyed the authority that came from being on top of things.

The diary of a woman who lived near Augusta, Georgia, provides a striking example not only of changing personal

28. *The Private Journal of Henry W. Ravenel,* ed. Arney Robinson Childs (Columbia, S.C.; University of South Carolina Press, 1947), p. 280.

29. *Southern Cultivator* 26: 207, cited by Bell I. Wiley in "Vicissitudes of Early Reconstruction Farming in the Lower Mississippi Valley," *Journal of Southern History* 3 (November 1937): 452.

fortunes but of the effect on a wife and mother. In 1855 she had noted:

I thank thee oh my Heavenly Father for thy many mercies, but for none do I sincerely thank thee as for *my husband,* combining such moral quality, such an affectionate heart, with just such a master will as suits my woman's nature, for true to my sex I delight *in looking up* and love to feel my woman's weakness protected by man's superior strength.[30]

But then this ideal husband went off to war. When he returned he tried to recoup his situation by planting on land much of which had come to him through his wife. His efforts were unavailing; he borrowed money and eventually was forced to sell out to pay debts, causing endless mortification to his wife. She and the children were often in actual want, and by 1870 she was writing, "I know that our children must be fed, clothed and educated and I hope by God's aid to assist in accomplishing that object." She thought of taking a job in town, decided instead to open a school, which she did, with some financial reward and much real pleasure. When the time came for summer vacation she was actually sorry, and not only because of the money that would not come in during the holiday. In her diary the comments about her husband became increasingly bitter through the years. His "superior strength," at least in the context of the postwar years, had turned out to be an illusion.

Defeat and postwar conditions in the South undermined the patriarchy. Slavery, which had provided the original need for the idea, was gone, and many men came home to

30. Diary of E. G. C. Thomas, MS Dept., Duke.

face conditions which proved unmanageable. Perhaps only on rich land, and with extraordinary managerial ability, would anyone have done well farming in the South in the first decade after the war. It might be argued, too, that the only men who succeeded in this difficult enterprise were those whose wives were able to contribute skill, energy, encouragement, and perhaps even a little outside income. Mrs. Clay, for example, did not help her husband, but spent her time traveling and mourning the lost past. Whatever the inherent difficulty of the situation, the result was that members of the superior sex, whom women had been taught to lean upon and look up to, were often notably unable to cope with the new life.

In April 1867 the Charleston Board of Trade held an anniversary meeting, at which, amidst much eating and drinking, a number of toasts were offered. The ninth was to Woman, and the reply to it was straight from the antebellum lexicon:

This is the true mission of woman: to elevate, to refine and to improve mankind. . . . The domestic circle, the school, the hospital, the bedside of suffering—these are the true sphere of woman. It is her mission to make home happy, to keep burning the lamp of religion, to teach men virtue. May that day never come when her beautiful nature shall be lowered to the arena of politics and party strife.[31]

What were women doing at the moment these words were being spoken? "Anything and everything we could to make a living," wrote Myrta L. Avary. Noting in passing that "some whose record for courage and steadiness on the field of battle reflects glory on our common country, failed ut-

31. Proceedings of the First Anniversary of the Charleston Board of Trade, Charleston, 1867, p. 30.

terly at adaptation," she went on to give eyewitness accounts of a North Carolina woman reduced to hitching herself to a plow driven by her eleven-year-old son and a Virginia woman driving a plow to which she had put her two daughters. "The great mass of Southern women," she concluded, "had to drop books for broomsticks, to turn from pianos and guitars and make music with kettles and pans. Children had to help. . . . the hour was strenuous beyond description." [32]

In one way or another the hour was to remain strenuous for a long time to come. Southerners had barely begun to pick up the pieces when they were flung into new turmoil by congressional reconstruction. This crisis channeled a great deal of masculine energy into politics and such capers as the Ku Klux Klan, putting an even greater burden on the women for the maintenance of everyday life. Then, when economic order was once again being slowly restored, came the depression of 1873.

It is not surprising, in the circumstances, to find some subtle changes taking place in the self-image of southern women. "Let me say," wrote one South Carolina matron, "that while my young life was somewhat shadowed, and I was cut off from the privileges of an education . . . still I am glad to have lived through a period like this, and believed that what there is in me of womanliness and strength of character and endurance is greatly due to the lessons of self-confidence . . . taught me during the war." [33]

32. Myrta L. Avary, *Dixie after the War,* pp. 157, 163, 297.
33. Mrs. James Hoyt, in Sallie E. Taylor, ed., *South Carolina Women in the Confederacy* 1 (Columbia, S.C.: United Daughters of the Confederacy, 1903): 371.

The journalists, observers and official emissaries who swarmed over the South after Appomattox usually had their eyes fixed on the freedmen and reserved their psychological probing for men lately in rebellion. But when their attention wandered for a moment they sometimes noticed something about the women.

It is a noteworthy ethnological fact, and one which I have often observed, that of the younger generation the southern women are much superior to the southern men both in intellect and energy; and their ascendancy over society is correspondingly great.[34]

"How superior the women of the South are to their brothers!" wrote Stephen Powers in 1868. "Whatever my opinion may be of the latter, for the former considering the domestic and literary education they have received I have the most profound respect."[35] Sidney Andrews decided that the "beauty of the South is solely in the faces of its young women," and Whitelaw Reid made a similar comment. All these were outsiders. Wilbur Fiske Tillett, a native southerner, looking back from the vantage point of 1891 concluded:

It was the heart, the hope, the faith of Southern womanhood that set Southern men to working when the war was over, and in this work they led the way, filling the stronger sex with utter amazement at the readiness and power with which they began to perform duties to which they had never been used before.

34. Benjamin Truman, reporting to President Andrew Johnson, Senate Executive Document 43, 39th Cong., 1st sess., 8 May 1866, p. 6.
35. *Afoot and Alone: A Walk from Sea to Sea* (Hartford: Columbian Book Co., 1872), p. 33.

He went on to ask the crucial question, "How then has Southern womanhood been affected by these great changes?" [36]

John Andrew Rice was speaking in hyperbole and with no particular regard for historical precision; yet his observation, formulated as a boy growing up in the nineties is interesting:

> In 1860 the South became a matriarchy. The men went away from home to other battlefields, leaving the women free to manage farm and plantation directly, without their bungling hindrance; when they returned, those who had escaped heroic death . . . they found their surrogates in complete and competent charge and liking it. Four years had fixed the habit of command, which, when I first began to know them, thirty had not broken, nor could they forget how pleasant life had been when all the men were gone.[37]

What inexperienced northern visitors called superiority, what southern observers glorified in traditional terms as the beneficent "influence" of southern ladies, what John Andrew Rice perceived as matriarchy, were all evidence that significant cultural patterns were changing. The knowledge, attitudes, and values shared by southerners, and the ideal patterns—the generally accepted view of how people *should* behave in certain situations were, bit by bit, being altered.

The war followed by Reconstruction marked the beginning of a widening gulf between the sexes, or some members of each, on the question of woman's appropriate role. The

36. Sidney Andrews, *The South since the War* (Boston: Ticknor & Fields, 1866), p. 40; Whitelaw Reid, *After the War* (New York: Moore, Wilstach & Baldwin, 1866); Wilbur Fiske Tillett, "Southern Womanhood as Affected by the War," *Century* 43 (1891): 9–16.

37. *I Came Out of the Eighteenth Century* (New York: Harper & Bros., 1942), pp. 116–17.

southern male self-image could hardly fail to be shaken when southern armies were defeated on the battlefield. John William DeForest, a Connecticut Yankee who had lived in Charleston for a time before the war, was sent to Greenville, South Carolina, with the Freedmen's Bureau. He had a novelist's eye for human types:

> It seems to me that the central trait of the "chivalrous Southron" is an intense respect for virility. He will forgive almost any vice in a man who is manly; he will admire vices, which are but exaggerations of the masculine. If you will fight, if you are strong and skillful enough to kill your antagonist, if you can govern or influence the common herd, if you can ride a dangerous horse over a rough country, if you are a good shot or an expert swordsman, if you stand by your own opinions unflinchingly, if you do your level best on whiskey, if you are a devil of a fellow with women, if, in short, you show vigorous masculine attributes he will grant you his respect. . . .
>
> It may be taken for granted that a people which so highly prizes virility looks upon man as the lord of creation and has old fashioned ideas as to what is the proper sphere of woman. If the high-toned gentleman continues to be influential at the South, it will be a long time before the "strong-minded" obtain much of a following there, a very long time before they will establish female suffrage.[38]

The picture is a familiar one, and DeForest's speculations about the speed with which female suffrage would arrive in the South were close to the mark. But what he did not go on to observe was that the experience of defeat would often sadly diminish the self-esteem of the "helluva fellow," and that the experience of self-sufficiency during the war had opened the door a crack to the "strong-minded" women.

38. *A Union Officer in Reconstruction* (New Haven: Yale University Press, 1948), p. 185.

For half a century southern women would be extolled for their contribution to the war, in images that owed a good deal to the antebellum female ideal. Francis W. Dawson's much quoted "Our Women in the War" may be taken as typical:

Who will undertake to describe adequately the exploits of our men in the war, and what was their mighty accomplishment in comparison with the infinite emprise of our women! The men, the soldiers, were the strong right arm, the mighty body of the Southern Confederacy, as with spirit undaunted they trod, with bleeding feet, the way of the Southern Cross. But as the men were the body, so the women were the soul. The men may forget the uniform they wore—it is faded and moth eaten today. But the soul, the spirit our women incarnate, cannot die. It is unchangeable, indestructible and, under God's providence, for our vindication and justification shall live forever! [39]

Thousands of Daughters of the Confederacy float before our eyes! But what Dawson, even in the eighties, married to a woman who had turned newspaper columnist after the war, did not comprehend was the thoroughgoing social change which the war had precipitated among southern women. And after the war came Reconstruction, a world they never made, but one with which they had to cope. It was in the Reconstruction period that the first foreshadowing of a new style of woman began to appear.

Functionally the patriarchy was dead, though many ideas associated with it lived on for years. Personality styles of southern women were changing to meet the changed time; the new patterns would become increasingly apparent as the century wore on.

39. P. 38.

Part two
THE "NEW WOMAN"

Girls who are growing up at the
present day ought not to compare
themselves with those of even
twenty years ago. Every year is
adding to their opportunities
and advantages. Door after door
is being flung open to them, and
the question must be . . .
which shall I enter? . . . with
the strongest conservative
principles it is impossible to
believe that women will continue
to move in the same narrow
ruts as heretofore.

Cornelia Phillips Spencer
in "The Young Ladies' Column,"
North Carolina Presbyterian, 1870

5

*Door
after Door
Is Being
Flung Open . . .*

S ignificant social changes have a way of taking place while people are looking the other way. Beyond the simple necessity of survival, public, and to a degree private, attention immediately after the war was fixed upon two things: the Negro and politics. As a consequence it was some time before many people noticed, or reflected upon, what was taking place in the "woman's sphere" of southern life.

In retrospect it is clear that many underlying conditions of women's lives had been significantly altered by the abolition of slavery and the widespread destruction of the plantation system. Also, in the postwar readjustment of the economy, towns were increasing in number and size. Poverty was everywhere, especially in the rural districts and in the areas that invading armies had entered. The war had created a generation of women without men. A quarter of a million men had died in the war, and afterward the tendency of young men to go west in search of a new start took an additional toll in the old southeastern states. The 1870 census recorded 25,000 more women than men in North Carolina, 36,000 in Georgia, 15,000 in Virginia, and 8,000 in South Carolina.[1]

As the census takers filled in their schedules in an old southern state like Georgia it might have seemed at first glance that nothing much had changed, especially in the rural areas. In one monotonous column after another men were listed as "farmer" or "farm laborer" and white females identified as "keeping home." A closer look would have revealed that many of these white females, though listed as

1. *Compendium of the Ninth Census* (Washington, 1873). As late as 1890 there were still 60,000 Confederate widows living in the South.

homemakers, perhaps in part fulfilling the census taker's expectation, were also heads of families, presiding over a farm and a family of teen-age boys and girls.

The bare identification of the census schedules revealed nothing about the changing demands of "keeping home" which had been brought about by the emancipation of slaves, or by the problems of credit, labor, and worn-out land which characterized postwar southern agriculture. Whatever new responsibilities they had acquired, women also carried on their traditional ones—gardening, taking care of cows and poultry, cooking and cleaning, watching over the crops when men were away, and supervising children. The lower the social level, the harder the woman's work. The significance of the female contribution to farm life was clearly recognized by the Grange when, sweeping over the South in the seventies, it offered membership to women on equal terms with men. The Farmers Alliance followed the same pattern, and in the nineties the Populist party subscribed to a national plank calling for woman suffrage.

It is impossible to know how many women were planting or farming on their own account, though the manuscript census returns suggest that there were many. A South Carolina editor noted that for years after the war his father planted in partnership with his mother-in-law, though he does not give any details. When Thomas Dabney, in his old age, gave up planting in Mississippi, one of his daughters assumed responsibility for the plantation. Elizabeth Allston Pringle, widowed in South Carolina, took up rice planting, preferring that life, with all its trials, to dependency. Fanny Kemble's daughter wrote an account of her own ten years in charge of the plantation which had led to her mother's disillusionment with the South before the war.[2] In Kentucky, Mrs. Cassius Clay, who came home from Russia because of her ambassador husband's adventures with Russian ladies, took over the family farm, paid off the debt, built a large house, and supported six children. In 1885 at the age of seventy she was still making a profit from her 350-acre farm.[3] Her daughter Laura, a spinster, also operated a successful farm.[4]

Not all women who worked as farmers or planters were officially the heads of families; many were wives left in charge of the farm or plantation by husbands engaged in law, medicine, or politics.[5] Tom Watson's wife, despite an appearance of fragile gentility, was "the business executive of several large farms, employing and discharging scores of tenants, keeping accounts, buying supplies, directing work, relieving her husband of a vast amount of routine." [6] Much the same could be said of many southern women of the time.

One of the talented daughters of a prewar senator from South Carolina had been raised in Columbia and was not especially fond of country living. At the end of the war she

2. William Watts Ball, *South Carolina, the State That Forgot* (Indianapolis: Bobbs-Merrill, 1932); Elizabeth Allston Pringle, *A Woman Rice Planter* (New York: Macmillan, 1913); Frances Butler Leigh, *My Ten Years on a Georgia Plantation* (London: R. Bentley, 1883).

3. Elizabeth Cady Stanton et al., *History of Woman Suffrage* (Rochester, N.Y., 1886), 3:820.

4. Clara Goodman, *Bitter Harvest* (Lexington: Bur Press, 1946), p. 34.

5. Ora Lewis Bradley, *The Country Doctor's Wife* (New York: House of Field, 1940), gives a good picture of the life of such a woman on a Georgia farm in the eighties and nineties. With all the necessary cooking, sewing, and caring for cows, chickens, and garden, the whole family, including the children, had to work hard just to do the daily tasks.

6. C. Vann Woodward, *Tom Watson: Agrarian Rebel* (New York: Macmillan, 1939), p. 46.

had no choice but to join her husband in an attempt to restore his burned and pillaged family plantation. She met the challenge with intelligence and skill, developed a wide reputation as a first-rate horse doctor, gave music and French lessons to bring in a little cash, sang in the choir to pay for her church pew, and laughed to herself about the supposed weakness of "ladies." An active member of both the Grange and the United Daughters of the Confederacy, she lived to write spirited memoirs in her nineties.[7]

Mrs. Mary Ross Banks of Macon, Georgia, widowed once by the war and again in 1879, decided there was no use relying upon anything but her own efforts. She took up farming successfully enough to support herself and her son and did a little writing on the side.[8] Perhaps the necessity for many women to assume responsibility for farms and plantations lay behind the recommendation of the trustees of the University of Alabama in 1871 that women be admitted to the "theoretical and practical horticultural classes." [9]

The town census schedules were less monotonous than those for the country. Here, too, many women were identified as "keeping home," but many others were listed as teachers, seamstresses, laundresses, boardinghouse keepers, and mill workers. A very large number of spinsters appeared in the returns, many living with relatives and said to have "no occupation." [10]

7. Sallie Elmore Taylor, Memoirs, SHC UNC.
8. Frances Willard and Mary A. Livermore, *American Women,* 2 vols. (New York: Mast, Crowell & Kirkpatrick, 1897), 1:52.
9. James B. Sellers, *History of the University of Alabama* (University, Ala., University of Alabama Press, 1953), 1: 474–75.
10. This summary is based on the 1870 manuscript census returns for six Georgia counties, including those encompassing Atlanta, Rome, and Athens.

The changes in women's occupations, reflected as early as the 1870 census, had begun during the war and were accelerated by the desperate need for work in the immediate postwar period. Any channel that opened was welcomed. The shortage of men who could take the loyalty oath, for example, made it possible for women to become postmistresses. Fannie Pender, the general's beautiful wife, widowed at twenty-three when he died at Gettysburg, was appointed postmistress at Tarboro, North Carolina, and pieced out her income by teaching school.[11] In 1866 the *Montgomery Advertiser* announced that it was willing to teach young ladies to set type.[12] A veteran just out of the Confederate navy, visiting his family in Memphis, found his sister in the process of buying a cotton gin as a means of self-support and meantime, or so he asserted, making $75 a month from a garden which she cultivated herself.[13]

The surge of interest in education which came after the war contributed significantly to the changing patterns of women's lives. There had never been much in the way of public education in the slave states, and what little there was had been destroyed by the war. Reconstruction constitutions included provision for public schools, and by the time the last Union soldier left the South, a growing number of native southerners were concluding that a greatly increased educational effort was essential if the economy was to be rebuilt and racial tensions ameliorated. What followed

11. William W. Hassler, ed., *The General to His Lady,* p. 262.

12. *New Orleans Daily Picayune,* 14 January, 25 February 1866, cited in Kathryn Reinhart Schuler, "Women in Public Affairs in Louisiana during Reconstruction," *Louisiana Historical Quarterly* 19 (January–October 1936): 668–750.

13. George W. Gift to Ellen Gift, May 1865, SHC UNC.

was a mammoth effort to build an educational system with inadequate resources and in the face of indifference, apathy, or outright resistance. Sometimes called the "educational revival," the movement had the overtones of a religious crusade. Outside help in the form of northerners who came to teach the freedmen, northern money, and earnest agents who gave their lives to proselyting supplemented the southern effort.[14]

The increasing interest in education coincided with the need of large numbers of women to find paid employment. Schoolteaching had always been a respectable thing to do, and now it was the first thought of many upper-class women who needed to earn money. The superintendent of public instruction for the state of Alabama told the Senate Committee on Education and Labor in 1883 that "members of the most elegant and cultivated families in the State are engaged in teaching." [15] A. D. Mayo, a Universalist minister who spent twelve years working for southern educational improvement, wrote in the early nineties that nothing had impressed him more than "the push to the front of the better sort of Southern young womanhood, everywhere encouraged by the sympathy, support, sacrifice, toils and pray-

14. The full story of the educational crusade may be found in Charles W. Dabney, *Universal Education in the South* (Chapel Hill: University of North Carolina Press, 1936); see also Rose H. Holder, *McIver of North Carolina* (Chapel Hill: University of North Carolina Press, 1957); Dumas Malone, *Edwin A. Alderman* (New York, 1940); E. A. Alderman and A. L. Gordon, *J. L. M. Curry* (New York: Macmillan, 1911); R. D. W. Connor and Clarence Poe, *Life and Letters of Charles B. Aycock* (Garden City, N.Y.: Doubleday, Page, 1912); Harnett T. Kane, *Miracle in the Mountains* (Garden City: Doubleday, 1956).

15. *Report of the Senate Committee on Education and Labor* (Washington, 1885), 48th Cong., 2d sess., 4: 203.

ers of the superior women of the elder generation at home." [16] And in 1902, G. Stanley Hall visited a teacher-training summer program at the University of Tennessee and commented that the southern teachers were from "the best walks of life." [17]

Whether women went into the fledgling public schools, opened their own little private schools, or taught in one of the seminaries and academies which had survived from the past, many of them felt their preparation for teaching to be inadequate. They were therefore ready to respond dramatically when the educational reformers organized summer institutes or summer normal schools. Even three-day teacher-training institutes were oversubscribed, so great was the felt need of improvement.[18]

The next logical step was a demand for regular teacher-training schools. George Peabody of Massachusetts helped finance a normal school which opened in Nashville in 1875 with thirteen young women among its students and two women on the faculty. By the end of the first year the enrollment had reached sixty and scholarships were being offered to women on equal terms with men.[19] In Mississippi, even before the war, a Grenada woman had persuaded the governor to recommend the establishment of a woman's college. When the war ended she renewed her efforts, and when she left the state in 1873 another woman took up the

16. A. D. Mayo, "Southern Women in the Recent Educational Movement in the South," *Bureau of Education Circular of Information,* no. 1 (Washington, 1892), pp. 38–39.

17. Quoted in Dabney, *Universal Education,* 2:112. Manuscript sources for these years are filled with references to young women schoolteachers. From these sources, it seems that half the young women in the postwar South must have taught school at least briefly.

18. Malone, *Alderman;* Holder, *McIver,* passim.

19. Dabney, *Universal Education,* 2:117.

cause. In 1884 the legislature finally agreed to establish the State Industrial Institute and College to give collegiate education, normal training, and industrial preparation to the young women of Mississippi. This was the first state-supported college for women in the United States.[20]

In Alabama, too, a woman headed the campaign which persuaded the legislature to found a normal and industrial school for girls—Julia Tutwiler, daughter of a well-known antebellum school man who as a student at the University of Virginia had taken his inspiration from Thomas Jefferson. Henry Tutwiler's Green Springs Academy had been one of the most respected in the state, and his daughter had taken advantage of what the academy afforded. After the war she went to a French boarding school in Philadelphia, spent a year at Vassar College, and went on to a teacher-training institute in Kaiserwirth, Germany. With this preparation she went back to Alabama to take charge of the Livingston Female Academy. In 1881 she persuaded the legislature to make a grant to her school for teacher training. With this beginning she began to organize a public campaign for a normal and industrial college, which the legislature agreed to in 1895.[21]

The North Carolina State Normal and Industrial School for Women, which opened in 1891 was primarily the creation of a man. Charles Duncan McIver was a member of a group of able young men who had been classmates at the University of North Carolina and had worked together in the leadership of the educational movement in that state. McIver was singularly devoted to the cause of women's edu-

20. Ibid., 1: 356.
21. Anne Gary Pannell and Dorothea E. Wyatt, *Julia Tutwiler* (University, Ala.: University of Alabama Press, 1961).

cation. His wife had been a schoolteacher and was apparently an unusually able woman. Perhaps she made him aware of the one-sided nature of what the state offered to its young, and of the loss to society when women did not have a chance for education. He campaigned across the state, and before the legislature, and when the school he advocated became a reality he was made its president.[22]

Small and inadequate though they were, these normal schools were extremely important. Coming into a vacuum, they had far-reaching influence. They offered the first systematic training to prepare women for remunerative work. While they were at the outset primarily vocational, they provided enough general education to awaken the interest and spur the ambition of able girls who sometimes then went on to northern schools. The teachers trained in these normal schools began to teach in the public schools and there helped create the clientele for the few women's liberal arts colleges which were beginning to develop in the South.[23] Bit by bit a little core of college-educated women was built up, whose influence belied their number. Among them could be found the first tiny group of lawyers, doctors, and college professors and from their ranks were drawn many of the leaders of community action in the years after 1890.

A milestone in this development was the organization in

22. Holder, *McIver,* passim.

23. A sensitive and illuminating account of what it was like to try to organize a first-class woman's college in the South may be found in Brandt V. B. Dixon, *A Brief History of the H. Sophie Newcomb Memorial College* (privately printed, 1928). "I was notified also," President Dixon writes, "that it was confidently expected that the students should finish the course at the age of seventeen. As this was somewhat less that I had fixed in my own mind as the proper age of admission, my discussion of this point was marked less by frankness than an effort at diplomacy" (pp. 25–26).

1903 of the Southern Association of College Women. Membership in this group was limited to women who had degrees from colleges of high standards, and many of the members were graduates of colleges and universities outside the South. In 1906 there were 334 members, nearly half with degrees from northern and western institutions. By 1913 there were nearly six hundred members, with degrees from twenty schools outside the South as well as from the four recognized women's colleges and some of the coeducational universities in the South.[24]

Widening educational opportunity affected women in many ways. As public schools slowly spread across the South, illiteracy declined and chances for the bright-but-poor girl to secure an education increased. At the same time every additional schoolroom created a new job for a woman, and by the turn of the century women schoolteachers constituted a growing cadre of professional women.

Some women seized this new opportunity in dramatic ways. In New Orleans a crippled girl, Sophie Bell Wright, began a little school around her mother's dining room table, with twenty pupils each paying fifty cents a month. Meantime she paid her way through the Peabody Normal Seminary by teaching math. In 1894 she began a night school for for working men and boys who were too poor to pay for education. By 1903 there were 1,500 students in the night school.[25] In the mountains of North Georgia a forceful

24. The outside colleges included Smith, Vassar, Wellesley, Bryn Mawr, Radcliffe, Michigan, and Swarthmore, among others. The four southern colleges which entitled a woman to membership were Agnes Scott, Goucher, Randolph-Macon, and Sophie Newcomb. Southern Association of College Women, *Sixth Report, 1909,* and *Proceedings in Full of the Tenth Annual Meeting* (Richmond, Va., 1913).

25. Margaret Evelyn Gardner, *Sophie Bell Wright,* M.A. thesis, L.S.U., 1959.

young woman began teaching a Sunday School for mountain children in an abandoned log cabin, from which developed the almost epic saga of the Berry Schools.[26]

Two women provide telling examples of the difference educational opportunity could make. Celeste Parrish was an orphan girl born in Virginia in 1853 and raised by maiden aunts, who were not inclined to pay for schooling for a girl. At sixteen she began teaching to support herself and, after a chance encounter with a book on the theory of teaching, decided that she was in dire need of training. She worked to put herself through the Virginia Normal School and from there moved on to study first mathematics and astronomy and later psychology at Michigan, Cornell, and Chicago. She taught for a while at Randolph-Macon, but her time at Chicago convinced her that John Dewey was on the right track about children's education. In 1900 she went to the Georgia State Normal School, where she supervised the development of a Dewey-style teacher-training school and introduced Georgia to progressive education. After years as head of the department of pedagogy at the Normal School, during which she helped train hundreds of teachers, she became supervisor of rural education in North Georgia, the first woman to hold such a post. In this capacity she traveled over the countryside in buggy and wagon carrying the gospel of education to backwoods parents.[27]

Julia Tutwiler, whose work for teacher training in Alabama has been mentioned, was roughly a contemporary of Celeste Parrish. In addition to her educational work Miss Tutwiler was also a one-woman conscience for her native

26. Kane, *Miracle in the Mountains*.
27. Mary E. Creswell, "Personal Recollections of Celeste Parrish," typescript in author's possession.

state. She led movements to abolish the noxious convict lease system, to reform the prisons generally, and to establish a training school for boys.[28]

Julia Tutwiler was born in 1841, Celeste Parrish in 1853. Had they been born thirty years earlier, each might have lived out her days as a maiden aunt or an unusually gifted governess for somebody's children. But growing up in the postwar years when the drive to educate children was taking shape and the barriers against career women giving way, each found a field to develop her unusual capacities. There were many others like them, spinsters nearly all. Times were changing but it was still usually necessary for a woman to choose between marriage and a demanding career.

Another kind of life style made possible by the opportunity for education was exemplified by Harriet Morehead Berry of North Carolina. Born in the old colonial capital of Hillsboro, Harriet Berry went to one of the well-known academies for girls, the Nash-Kollock School. In 1893 she became one of the early matriculants at the North Carolina Normal and Industrial School at Greensboro. For a few years after graduation she taught in a school for orphans, but finding this did not provide the satisfaction she expected, she went back to Greensboro to take the business course. As the leading student in her class she was recommended for a position as stenographer to the State Geological and Economic Survey. Here she made herself an expert on the economic resources and opportunities of North Carolina. It was clear to her that a rural state without a good port, stretching seven hundred miles from east to west, needed above all a good system of roads. Later, as executive

28. Pannell and Wyatt, *Julia Tutwiler.*

secretary of the Good Roads Association, she became the chief person working for a state-supported road network in North Carolina, and when the program was finally adopted it was unanimously agreed that Harriet Berry was largely responsible.[29]

Although teaching absorbed the largest number of upper-class single women in search of employment, there were other ways of earning a living, some more demanding than others. The number of women who took to the pen as a means of livelihood suggests that there was a considerable demand for sentimental fiction.

Augusta Evans, who had toyed briefly with the idea of writing a secret history of the Confederacy, turned back to her more accustomed novel writing, and her *St. Elmo,* published in 1866, removed any fear of poverty forever. A few of these late nineteenth-century southern women writers can still be read with pleasure and profit—Grace King, Kate Chopin, Mary N. Murphree, perhaps—but the work of hundreds of others is, happily, buried in the back pages of newspapers, in regional literary magazines, or in moldy volumes long since out of print. Not only did a large number of women see themselves as literary artists but many women active in other fields—farming, temperance, teaching—wrote poems and stories on the side. What southern literature lacked in quality it made up in quantity.[30]

29. Harriet Morehead Berry Papers, SHC UNC.
30. See the biographical essays in Willard and Livermore, *American Women,* for sketch after sketch of these self-styled "writers" and "poets" and for the writing habits of temperance workers, schoolteachers, and almost any other literate female. See also Mary E. Tardy, *Living Female Writers of the South* (Philadelphia: Clayton, Remsen & Haffelfinger, 1870).

A good many women became newspaper editors. Eliza Frances Andrews, whose youthful journal provides a classic picture of adolescence in wartime, reported that in 1873 she had found it necessary to earn a living, "though wholly unprepared either by nature or training for a life of self-dependence." She wasted no time in regret but took over the editorship of a country newspaper, the man hired to do the job giving her half his salary while she did all the work. When the supposed editor found a better job, he recommended Miss Andrews as his successor, but the proprietor declared that it would be impossible for a woman to fill such a position. Even when informed that she *had* filled it with some success for six months, he was unmoved. Miss Andrews went on to teach school, write articles for the northern press, publish novels and plays, and train herself in botany to the point that she could write two successful texts in the field and admit to being the best field botanist in the South.[31]

Other women journalists were equally spirited. Eliza Jane Poitevent, born in 1849, published, under the pseudonym of Pearl Rivers, poetry which attracted the attention of the editor of the *New Orleans Picayune*. He not only published the poetry but married the poet. She became increasingly active in the editorial management of the paper, and when her husband died she took complete charge. Her second marriage, to the co-owner, did not diminish her influence, and the *Picayune* was not only the largest paper in the country edited by a woman, but a vehicle for Eliza Poite-

31. Eliza Frances Andrews, *Wartime Journal of a Georgia Girl* (New York, D. Appleton, 1908), pp. xiv–xvii; Willard and Livermore, *American Women*, 1: 26.

vent Nicholson's public concerns, which were many. She welcomed women to her staff, "discovered" Elizabeth Meriwether Gilmer, who invented the Dorothy Dix advice column, and gave good newspaper coverage to the work of New Orleans women.[32]

The list of southern women newspaper editors is long. Among the more interesting was one Elia Good Byington, who had been born in Thomaston, Georgia, in 1858. With her husband she was joint proprietor of the *Columbus* (Georgia) *Evening Ledger,* and her crusading zeal for women's rights led her to hire women for all jobs on the paper, except those of carrier boy and four men who did "outdoor work." There was a woman foreman, as well as women typesetters, proofreaders, and reporters.[33] Mary Ann Thomas of Springfield, Tennessee, was editor, publisher, clerk, and proofreader of the *Record* and raised a family at the same time.[34] Florence Williams, born in Bryan County, Georgia, in 1865, left home at sixteen to do battle with the world. In 1889 she took charge of the *Statesboro Eagle* and did all the work on the paper while contributing also to a literary magazine. In 1892 she established a news and literary paper in Valdosta. Still another woman established and edited the *Sherman* (Texas) *Daily Democrat,* and in Huntsville, Alabama, the daughters of Withers Clay took over the *Democrat* of that town when their father became ill in 1884

---

32. *Dictionary of American Biography,* S. V. "Nicholson, Eliza Jane Poitevent Holbrook"; Harnett T. Kane, *Dear Dorothy Dix* (Garden City, N.Y.: Doubleday, 1952). For southern women 1849 was a vintage year; a number of those who appear in these pages were born then. This meant of course that they were just sixteen when the war ended, and coming to womanhood precisely at the moment when southern ladies were beginning to move into new patterns.

33. Willard and Livermore, *American Women* 1:143.

34. Ibid. 2: 710–11.

and continued to edit it until 1919. Miss Addie McGrath ran the *Baton Rouge Truth*.[35]

Among these journalists were some who published papers primarily devoted to women's rights. There was such a paper in St. Petersburg, called *The Woman Question,* and one in Little Rock named *The Woman's Chronicle.* A similar publication in Liberty, Mississippi, called the *Advocate* was edited by a woman with the interesting name of Piney Woods Forsyth.[36]

Perhaps the most startling development of all in the realm of woman's work was the rapid movement of women into manual labor and factory work of various kinds. When the Senate Committee on Education and Labor held hearings in the South in the early eighties, the senators were told repeatedly about the many women workers in the mills.[37]

Clare DeGraffenried, a trained social investigator as well as a southerner, wrote in 1893 that poor white women were flocking to mills, laundries, and seamstress jobs and that

higher grade Southerners seek employment, over against the family wish, at clerking, dressmaking, patent medicines, binderies, textiles, box and cigarette factories . . . earning enough to lessen the pinch of poverty. Tobacco affords a lucrative pursuit without odium . . . and in a model Richmond factory the cigarette girl equals the best Northern workers in position, manners and education. Nowhere else in the world do so many well-bred women, bankrupt and bereft of male providers, labor at manual callings as in the South, pursuing

35. Nuremberger, *Clays of Alabama* p. 317; Annie N. Meyer, ed., *Woman's Work* (New York: H. Holt and Co., 1891), p. 133.

36. *New Orleans Daily Picayune,* 25 August 1869, 5 June 1872.

37. *Report of the Senate Committee on Education and Labor* (Washington, 1885), 4: 493, 538 ff.

without loss of caste vocations which elsewhere would involve social ostracism.[38]

Some years later, testifying before the United States Industrial Commission 7 April 1899, Miss DeGraffenried said that she had found girls who were high school graduates at work in textile mills in Charleston, because there were so few opportunities for women in the South, a situation which she thought was on the verge of changing.

As early as 1886 Orra Langhorne, a maverick Virginia lady who wrote on labor and racial problems, had made a similar observation in Lynchburg. There had been, she said, a very great need for occupations in which white women could support themselves, and in consequence "hundreds of them have been slaves to the sewing machine, working hard at unwholesome employment for very small pay." She thought the situation was improving, however, since the cigarette factories were employing three hundred white girls of all ages, from children of eight to "settled" women of twenty-five or thirty. Married women were not accepted. The workers, she said, came from all classes of society: "More than one refined lady, whose connections are to be found among the FFV's [First Families of Virginia], is earning better wages at the cigarette factory than she can make at the sewing machine." [39]

In 1881 a Woman's Social and Industrial Association was incorporated at New Orleans for the purpose of encouraging and helping working women. Four years later the New

38. Clare DeGraffenried, "The Condition of Wage Earning Women," *Forum* 15 (March 1893): 73–74.
39. Orra Langhorne, *Southern Sketches from Virginia 1881–1901,* ed. Charles E. Wynes (Charlottesville: University of Virginia Press, 1964), pp. 73–74.

Orleans Woman's Club was organized, with half its membership made up of self-supporting women and its major
purpose to help such women market their wares and their
skills, as well as acquire new skills. In addition to self-help
training programs, the Woman's Club ran an employment
bureau which in 1887–88 placed women as teachers, librarians, stenographers, typists, bookkeepers, governesses, music
teachers, canvassers, agents, collectors, nurses, housekeep-
ers, dressmakers, cashiers, and saleswomen. The head of
the bureau believed that there was plenty of work available
for trained women. Newspaper reports about the New Orleans Woman's Club in the eighties indicated not only that
working women were increasingly common but also that
they were—if the attitude of the press is any indication—increasingly admired.[40]

In 1890 the Eleventh Census made some comparisons of
the number of women in various occupations over a twenty-
year period. The census categories of agricultural and
domestic workers must have included large numbers of
Negro women. The professional, trade and transportation,
and manufacturing categories, by contrast, probably contained mostly white women. The figures suggest the changes
which were taking place. In Virginia, for example, the total
of 5,000 women in manufacturing in 1870 doubled by 1890,
though the total population had increased by less than a
third. In Mississippi 700 professional women were counted
in 1870, and over 3,000 in 1890; a fourfold increase in a
population which had increased only by 25 percent. Georgia
had 5,000 women in manufacturing and mechanical jobs in
1870, and 12,000 in 1890; and so it went in the whole South.

40. Scrapbook of the New Orleans Woman's Club, Dept. of MS,
Tulane.

The same census offered some calculations of the percentages of white females over ten who were gainfully employed. These ranged from a low of 5 percent in Texas to a high of 16 percent in South Carolina. By comparison, the figures for Massachusetts were 18 percent, for Pennsylvania 12 percent, and for Ohio and Illinois 10 percent. Aso by comparison, 30 percent of Negro women in Virginia were gainfully employed and 43 percent in Georgia.[41]

The professional women who turned up in the census in such rapidly increasing numbers included a handful of doctors and lawyers (though women were still prohibited from practicing law in many southern states), but the majority were teachers. In an undated newspaper column which appears to have been published in the eighties, Elizabeth Lyle Saxon reported with approbation the presence of young women architects and engineers in Memphis and rejoiced, a bit prematurely, "What a stride in twenty years. . . . No need now to marry for a home . . . no longer a drone in the home and the world, no longer a gossip but a well-educated, trained, human being." [42]

The changing pattern of women's work had begun as a condition, not a theory, growing out of hard times, the shortage of men, and the desperate need of women to support themselves and their children. But as the change began to be obvious, it was natural that a good deal of discussion of its significance should take place. As early as June 1875 the *New Orleans Picayune* published a series of varying opinions on the subject. There was emphasis on the great

41. All figures are round numbers based on the *Report on Population,* Eleventh Census, Part II (Washington, 1897).
42. Lyle Saxon Papers, Dept. of MS, Tulane.

number of women needing work, one correspondent going so far as to speak of "the sorrowful condition of Southern ladies." There was a good deal of support for permitting women to be retail clerks, though one conservative man thought only middle-aged women with families to support and maiden ladies who were clearly not in the marriage market should be eligible, and that both should dress modestly and pay strict attention to duty.[43]

Cornelia Phillips Spencer of Chapel Hill, North Carolina, devoted a great deal of thought to the same question. In 1871 she wrote:

> That a change must come, and that soon, in the kind of work allotted to woman among us, is self-evident. Our women are stretching out their hands imploring for work—work to aid a widowed mother—work to enable me to educate my younger brothers and sisters—work to save me from ignoble dependence—work to assist my overworked husband—what can I do? These are some of the appeals that have come to me within a few months past. . . . "There seems to be nothing we can do," writes a friend . . . "if we cannot teach, or make shirts, we must starve."
>
> . . . Communications are therefore solicited from intelligent women who feel an interest in woman's work.[44]

A year later she was suggesting that nine out of ten of the "insolent and underbred young men" in dry goods stores be sent to the fields and their places filled by "courteous and sensible" young women, adding:

> However, there is little likelihood of this change being effected shortly, because in it we would need the cooperation of

43. Schuler, "Women in Public Affairs in Louisiana during Reconstruction," p. 705.
44. "The Young Ladies' Column," *North Carolina Presbyterian,* 11 January 1871.

men, and the men of North Carolina, or anywhere else in the South, are not bothering their minds about woman's wants. What we can do we must do ourselves—we must assist each other.[45]

In successive issues of Mrs. Spencer's column in the *North Carolina Presbyterian* it is possible to watch a gradual evolution in the opinions of a woman brought up in the old regime who was nevertheless alert to the needs of the new. Mrs. Spencer's own "sphere" expanded steadily. Immediately after the war she went to work on a book, *The Last Ninety Days of the War in North Carolina,* in which she tried to record recent events as accurately as possible for the benefit of posterity. It was published in 1866. By that time her advice was already being sought, as it would be for thirty years, by leading public men in the state and key officials of the University of North Carolina, as well as by students who boarded at her table and were influenced by her opinions. Her behind-the-scenes efforts were credited with saving the university from near disaster during the Radical Reconstruction and reopening it to students.

By 1874 she was writing:

I am willing to reform by a gradual and gentle process many things which I once believed were meant by God to be immutable. And the position of my sex is one. There are many employments, many interests in life heretofore denied women which I cannot but think she has a right now to take up if she will. . . . To keep women at the same stand-point, occupied by the grandmothers of this generation, would be as unprofitable as it is impracticable. They have come to the front, forced there by other movements which they neither anticipated nor are responsible for, nor fully comprehend.[46]

45. Ibid., 31 January 1872.
46. Ibid., 22 April 1874.

Clare DeGraffenried, like Mrs. Spencer a southern lady, at age sixteen the first honor graduate of Wesleyan Female College in Georgia, had gone at twenty-seven to be a teacher in Washington. She moved into the ranks of the early social investigators and was a pioneer student of the working conditions of children and women. She, too, gave much thought to women and work and in 1890 suggested that

the advancement of women depends as largely upon those women who earn their bread by the sweat of their brow, as upon the education and training of idlers or students or even homemakers and care-takers. Women in business life are the entering wedge which will cleanse custom of prejudice and make a wider range possible for female effort.[47]

The Grange, which was primarily concerned with problems of farmers, brought at least one woman to a consideration of the issues touching on women's work. Sallie Elmore Taylor went to a national convention of the Grange where, she said, "I came on ideas . . . of women in relation with business affairs; wages, work, occupations of which I had no experience . . . the competition with men, the compensation for woman's and man's labor of the same grade and kind. The world's women dawned upon me, the women beyond and outside the prayer meeting . . . and home."[48]

In 1890 Wilbur Fiske Tillett of Vanderbilt undertook to write an article, "Southern Womanhood as Affected by the War," and had the notion of conducting a poll. His sample was small (five women and one man) but his questions were important ones. Those most relevant here were: "What

47. Clare DeGraffenried, "What Do Working Girls Owe to One Another," *Discussions of the Convention of Association of Working Girls Societies* (New York, 1890), p. 75.
48. Memoirs, SHC UNC.

change if any has taken place in woman's attitude toward work and self support, and in public sentiment with reference to this question?" "Can the southern white woman work now, without forfeiting her social standing, in the way in which the public sentiment of ante-bellum times would discount her social standing if she engaged in such work or self-support? What of the number and kinds of vocations open to women then and now and the pay given her for her work?"

On the answers to these questions especially, the members of his sample were in agreement. "Brothers and male relatives never used to suffer female members of their families to toil," wrote one woman, "as seems a matter of course now. If woman must struggle for self-support, it is delightful to contemplate the many avenues opening up to her whereby a livelihood may be gained." "You ask," wrote another, " 'What of the respectability of self-support? . . .' I answer that in the two cities with which I am familiar the most popular women in society are self-supporting women." The third, agreeing that single women were expected to earn a living, added with a degree of realism, "No matter what work a woman does, men will not pay her its full value, not half what they would pay a man for the very same work." A college professor, the only man in the sample, said that fully 25 percent of his women students expected to support themselves when they finished college.[49]

Most discussions of working women were concerned with the middle-class spinster, widow, or woman whose marriage had failed, who was teaching, doing office work, or, in some instances, training herself for a profession. Husbands of

49. Wilbur Fiske Tillett, "Southern Womanhood as Affected by the War," *Century* 48 (1891): 9–16.

middle-class women for the most part expected to support their wives. Some women, however, managed to define "helpmate" in fairly innovative ways; jointly edited papers, jointly run schools and orphanages were not uncommon. One woman listed among her accomplishments that she had been "counselor" to her husband.

By the turn of the century a significant percentage of southern females, especially single ones drawn from all social classes, and especially in the older states, were gainfully employed. An increasing number were entering the professions. Schoolteaching had almost become a woman's preserve as had jobs based on the new skills of typing and stenography. In the rural areas, the old patterns persisted, but girls who did not like them could go to work in a town, get a job in a mill, or even attend a normal or industrial school and prepare themselves to teach.

The movement of women into the world of gainful employment was born of necessity and of changing economic conditions. It is possible to argue that when the factories needed cheap labor, it became acceptable for women to work in mills; when businesses needed secretaries, when children needed teachers, whenever and wherever economic imperatives existed, mores and social barriers gave way.

It is also clear, however, that while many women worked from necessity and would happily have returned to dependency had any opportunity appeared, others found lasting satisfaction in independence. An early example was a young South Carolina woman who began teaching during the war. When it was over and the family was beginning to reestablish itself, her parents demanded that she give up her job and come home. After some discussion the daughter refused, adding, "I have made up my mind to one thing. I will hereafter act upon my own judgment. . . . I will not be a dependent old maid at home with an allowance doled out to me when I could be made comfortable by my own exertions." [50] Another young woman who had expressed the desire to teach before the war and been resolutely opposed by her parents found their opposition melting in the general desolation following the war. She, too, found the work itself satisfying, and when her husband was invalided she was able to support her own family and give help to younger brothers and sisters.[51] A woman reflecting, after a good many years of struggle, upon her decision to become a rice planter, concluded that she much preferred making her own living, as she had done for all her adult life except for the six years of a brief marriage, to assuming the care and responsibility of the hundreds of Negroes who would have been hers but for Emancipation.[52] Kate Cumming, who had discovered the satisfactions of work in wartime hospitals, never married but taught school and gave music lessons in Birmingham until her death in 1909. A mother and daughter who had fallen on hard times in Kentucky secured government jobs in Washington, one in the Post Office and one in the Land Office. They took rooms in a boardinghouse, and lived frugally on their government paychecks. For the mother, each day was a fresh struggle to dress, go to work, copy all day, and return home exhausted. The daughter found the experience of working interesting, though she rejoiced that her office was entirely made up of women so

50. Elizabeth Grimball to Meta Morris Grimball, 8 December 1866, Grimball Papers, SHC UNC.

51. Willard and Livermore, *American Women* 1: 42.

52. Elizabeth Allston Pringle, *Chronicles of Chicora Wood*, p. 8.

that she could dress comfortably and even remove her corsets in hot weather.[53] Clare DeGraffenreid, drawing on her wide observations as a social investigator as well as on her own experience, thought that most women either were dependent on a man or wanted to be, but she was sure that when the opportunity to earn a living was assured, any woman would be able "better to develop her own special gifts of womanhood; and whether married or single, the ability to maintain herself honorably whenever she chooses is essential to her dignity and freedom." [54]

Laura Clay, whose primary "career" was as a volunteer in the suffrage movement, also ran her own farm. In 1887 speaking to the Association for the Advancement of Women she developed her thoughts about women and work. She felt that the greatest disadvantage under which women suffered was that they were "not trained up to earn an independent living. . . . there is no true liberty when one is dependent upon the will of others for the means of subsistence." She pointed out that whatever might be the case in theory, in practice many women did not have men who could support them, and yet it was generally thought that girls did not need to be educated to earn a living. She deplored loveless marriages entered into solely for support and argued that a woman who worked before marriage was much better prepared for the arduous duties of wife, mother, and housekeeper.[55]

The president of the New Orleans Woman's Club, inaugurating its fifth year, commented in somewhat the same

53. Susan and Virginia Grigsby letters in the Gibson-Humphries Papers, SHC UNC.
54. "What Do Working Girls Owe to One Another," p. 78.
55. "The Responsibility of Women to Society," Paper read at Association for the Advancement of Women, Annual Congress, New York, 1887.

vein on the number of women who had, with the help of the
club, become self-supporting, ". . . their lives receiving a
new impulse through congenial employment, their homes
happier for their own more satisfied lives, growing daily
more harmonious." Her conclusion was precisely that of
Laura Clay—that every effort should be bent toward increasing educational opportunity so that more women could
find satisfaction in useful work.[56]

Eliza Frances Andrews, whose experiences in self-support
have been described earlier, put her thoughts on the whole
question of women's work into a novel published in 1879.
The heroine was a beautiful, talented, scholarly woman
burdened with a dissolute older brother and a foolish younger one. It became clear that she must take upon herself the
responsibility for maintaining the family. The developing
story was interlarded with a considerable amount of discussion about the limited number of jobs open to women and
the poor pay they received for the same work as men.
Though the heroine was determined to make her own way
instead of taking the easy way of marrying a rich man who
was eager for her hand, the author took care to provide her,
in the end, with a husband who accepted her radical views
and was willing to let her work.[57]

For many older women, work remained through their
lives a grim necessity. For the generation growing up after
1865 things were somewhat different. Virginia Meriwether

56. Scrapbook of the New Orleans Woman's Club, Dept. of MS,
Tulane.
57. [Eliza Frances Andrews], Elzey Hay, pseud., *A Mere Adventurer*
(Philadelphia: J. B. Lippincott, 1879), pp. 25–31, 43, 168–69. Though
Miss Andrews can hardly be called subtle, the chapter on Mildred's
decision to build a career in journalism is a firm statement of the virtues
of work for women.

was born in Memphis in 1862, the daughter of a woman who late in life would become a leading temperance and suffrage worker. A biographical sketch published in 1897 noted "heredity and education made simple to her a problem which had been complex to the generation before, and she took personal independence naturally. . . . Shortly after becoming a widow she went to New York to study medicine."[58] Obviously the problem had not been "made simple" for every woman, but the nature and meaning of women's work had changed radically in one generation. Not only had the number of respectable occupations multiplied, but the idea that any woman who could find a male relative to support her should do so was losing its force, as was the notion that for a woman independence was only acceptable when it was a grim necessity. The opportunity for earning money and attaining independence had as much to do with shaping the life style of the "new woman" as the necessity for it. Clare DeGraffenried summed it up:

In a general sense labor in search of an independent support broadens female character and supplies an interest in favor of intellectual development. When women are forced into new spheres, or voluntarily choose callings hitherto barred to the sex, they grow in versatility and self-reliance, and are also stimulated by their new duties to master, with eager delight, subjects formerly unattractive. For the creation of intellectual interests, the worker is always more favorably environed than the stay-at-home.[59]

58. Willard and Livermore, *American Women* 1: 235.
59. Clare DeGraffenried, "Working Mothers and Uncared for Children," *The Congregationalist* 12 May 1892, p. 6.

Southern women by education
and training are eminently
conservative. This movement was
new—startling. Many stood
aloof, watching it, ready to seize
upon any possible mistake or
innovation of woman's prescribed
sphere; but the leaven of the
Holy Spirit was working silently.

Tenth Annual Report of
the Woman's Missionary
Society of the Methodist
Episcopal Church South, 1888

6

The Lord Helps Those . . .

Spinsters, widows, wives with disabled husbands—such women had to earn a living, and the obviousness of their need protected them from criticism. But many town-dwelling middle-class wives had husbands well able to support them. In the on-rushing industrialization of the late nineteenth century many of the traditional economic tasks which nearly all women had performed in the recent rural past disappeared from the home. The story is too familiar to require repetition: smaller families, better health, canned food, ready-made clothes, all combined to reduce the time required for traditional household functions, and to expand leisure time, especially of urban wives. The presence of many Negro women willing to work for very low wages reduced still further the work of many wives and mothers. A certain psychological malaise accompanied these economic changes. One woman wrote: "Women who had been fully occupied with the requirements of society and the responsibilities of a dependency of slaves, were now tossed to and fro amidst the exigencies and bewilderments of strange and for the most part painful circumstances, and were eager that new adjustments should relieve the strained situation and that they might find out what to do." [1]

In the 1830s Alexis de Tocqueville had observed what he took to be a unique tendency. "Americans of all ages, all conditions, and all dispositions constantly form associations. . . . If it is proposed to inculcate some truth or to foster some feeling by the encouragement of a great example, they form a society." [2] It is not to be wondered at, therefore, that when American women began after the Civil War to search for self-improvement and then for community improvement,

1. Caroline Merrick, *Old Times in Dixie Land,* p. 172.
2. *Democracy in America* (New York: A. Knopf, 1944), 2: 106.

they founded voluntary associations. In the 1870s came the rapid growth of missionary societies, in the 1880s of the WCTU, and in the 1890s women's clubs. All three stemmed from a common impulse to learn about and begin to deal with the world outside the home.

In direct contradiction to the old saw about Satan finding work for idle hands, it was the firm conviction of many women that if their families needed them less, the Lord had work for them to do. An energetic Alabama woman foreshadowed the future when she wrote Bishop James Andrew in 1861, pointing to the immense amount of war work southern women were then engaged upon and saying that surely women loved God as much as country, if only the church would offer equally specific tasks to be done.

Here and there women's missionary societies had existed long before the war. At the first Baptist convention in 1823, when Alabama was still a frontier, half the delegates represented missionary societies, and, "Stranger still, every one of these missionary societies was a little organization of women that had been formed in obscurity, none knowing of the existence of any other, and thus without concert of action."[3] A female missionary society in Columbus, Mississippi, was said to have been in continuous existence since 1838, but before the war it had always sent a man as its delegate to various conventions.[4] The records of these early societies are fragmentary and thus the societies themselves are only dimly remembered.

What came to pass in the 1870s was of a different order of

3. B. F. Riley, *A Memorial History of the Baptists of Alabama* (Philadelphia: Judson Press, 1923), pp. 35–36.

4. Z. T. Leavell and T. J. Bailey, *A Complete History of Mississippi Baptists* (Jackson, Miss.: Mississippi Baptists Publishing Co., 1904), 2: 1415.

magnitude. Methodist, Baptist, and Presbyterian women all over the South were seized with a simultaneous impulse. They organized missionary societies, studied geography, raised money, and recruited people to go to remote parts of the globe.

Most southern churches took a conservative view of woman's role. Their publications were full of praise for ladylike women and expressions of horror at "unsexed" females. The erudite *Quarterly Review* of the Methodist Episcopal Church South examined the question "May Women Preach?" and stood firmly with Saint Paul, who was presumed to have forbidden it. The writer concluded that great caution was needed "in utilizing the gifts and graces of pious, zealous and intelligent women. Nothing can compensate for the sacrifice of feminine modesty: this must be guarded though the heavens fall!" [5]

Baptists editors agreed, and their opinions did not change much with the passing of decades. In 1868 the Baptist *Religious Herald* asserted: "As the rival of man, in the struggle for place, power and prominence, she, as the 'weaker vessel,' is doomed to defeat. From such a contest, she must inevitably come forth, not with modesty, delicacy and loveliness which impart a charm and influence to her sex, but soiled, dishonored and disappointed." [6] Thirty-one years later the same paper was saying: "When . . . woman becomes *emancipated* from the care of the young and the making of the home, she has entered into the worst of all bondage, which comes always to every one who disregards the law of his own life. They only 'walk at liberty' who have learned to obey the divine precepts, as written in their

5. July 1881, pp. 478–88.
6. 20 February 1868, p. 2.

being." [7] It was no wonder that one Mississippi Baptist woman, praying for the enlightenment of the heathen, added to her prayer, "I pray God to enlighten the minds of our benighted husbands and show them their error." [8]

Yet these same Baptists, while officially opposing women's rights in any form, encouraged women to work in benevolent causes and to participate in the temperance crusade "as long as these efforts remain dissociated from the feminist agitation and politics." [9] The Methodists, too, were happy to turn over to women not only the responsibility for raising money for foreign missions, but also for furnishing and taking care of parsonages and for supervising local philanthropy. In meeting these responsibilities the women gained a new sense of their own competence and some ultimately found themselves ready to take part in the feminist movement which the church so deplored. Later they would demand more power within the church itself. The church fathers who gave women new responsibilities were not as foresighted as a certain antebellum minister who had refused permission for a woman's prayer meeting on the ground that if the women were alone, "who knows what they would pray for?"

This growing tendency of women to form themselves into religious societies appeared in all denominations. The introspective search for salvation of the early days of the century turned outward. A missionary spirit directed itself both to foreign lands and to social problems at home.

When groups of women began to realize that societies like

7. 5 January 1899, p. 1.

8. Leavell and Bailey, *Complete History,* p. 1417.

9. R. W. Sapin, "Attitudes and Reactions of Southern Baptists on Social Issues, 1865–1890," Ph.D. diss., Vanderbilt University, 1961, p. 357.

their own were appearing in many places, they thought of combining all the southern societies into one organization for greater effectiveness. Methodists were the first to take this step. In 1878 the Southern Methodist General Conference, after some debate, authorized a Woman's Board of Foreign Missions; at the close of the year the board counted 218 societies, 5,890 members, $4,000 in the treasury, and one missionary in China. Ten years later it encompassed 2,399 societies, 56,783 members, and missionaries in dozens of places. In this fast-growing organization women learned how to administer programs and handle large sums of money. By 1890 the Methodist Woman's Board of Foreign Missions owned almost two hundred thousand dollars worth of property, and had responsibility for ten boarding schools, thirty-one day schools, and a hospital.[10] Three years later membership in the organization had risen to 76,000. Some women offered themselves as missionaries, and these, when they returned home or sent home reports, gave impetus to the movement. Foreign missions were an ideal place for women of courage and independence for whom the extraordinary challenge of living and working in a foreign culture was exhilarating.[11]

The Baptist church was slower to come around. Baptist ministers opposed any general southern women's organization for fear it would become a front for dangerous feminism. "An independent organization of women," wrote the Reverend Tiberius Jones of Virginia, "naturally tends toward a violation of divine interdict against a woman's

10. Twelfth Annual Report, Woman's Board of Foreign Missions, Methodist Episcopal Church South, Nashville, 1891.
11. See Noreen Tatum, *Crown of Service* (Nashville: Parthenon Press, 1960), especially pp. 199–220, on women missionaries to the Congo.

becoming a public religious teacher." [12] It was 1888 before Baptist women were strong enough to insist on their right to a federation and to secure authorization for it over male opposition. Until then they carried on within their local missionary societies the same kinds of programs as their Methodist sisters.

The mushrooming of church organizations had consequences beyond the number of missionaries supported, schools founded, or hospitals inaugurated in foreign lands. For many married women church work was the essential first step toward emancipation from their antebellum image of themselves and of "woman's sphere." In 1879 a prominent North Carolina minister assured his daughter that membership in a missionary society would be "no compromise of female modesty and refinement." [13]

Like the North Carolina minister, the men who encouraged the women did not foresee the psychological consequence of the door they opened. The historians of South Carolina Presbyterianism remarked that at the beginning women in the missionary society were so shy that they could only recite the Lord's Prayer in unison. They soon grew bolder. They progressed to sentence prayers, delivered seriatim, until finally more than half of them were willing to lead the prayer. [14] The South Carolina Methodist Women's Missionary Society was the first public meeting in the state to be presided over by a woman—this in 1880. "With experience and a growing and compelling sense of mission, women

12. *Minutes of Virginia Baptist Association, 1888,* p. 42.
13. A. W. Plyler, *The Iron Duke of the Methodist Itinerancy* (Nashville: Cokebury Press, 1925), p. 166.
14. F. D. Jones and W. H. Mills, eds., *History of the Presbyterian Church in South Carolina since 1850* (Columbia, S.C.,: R. L. Bryan, 1926), p. 442.

in the church began to gain confidence and slowly emerge from the self-consciousness and fear which bound them," observed the historian of Methodist women.[15] The public life of nearly every southern woman leader for forty years began in a church society. "The struggle that it cost the women to attain to the ultimate goal, in satisfaction of a conviction that the right was theirs to labor for the Lord, only served to qualify them the more for greater success, when once the end sought was reached," concluded a perceptive historian of the Alabama Baptists.[16]

As women gained self-confidence and felt pride in their achievements they asked for more independence and greater rights within the church structure. In 1902 the members of the Woman's Board of Home Missions petitioned the General Conference of the Methodist church to create the office of deaconess, an office for women which had developed in Europe and in certain northern denominations. This request led to a long, acrimonious debate in which it was argued that if women were given such an office they would begin to aspire to the ministry, which was unthinkable. One delegate went so far as to call the suggestion heresy. The women stood their ground and won their point, though a large group of ministers remained unconvinced.[17]

Another bitter battle took place in the Methodist church in 1906, when, without consulting the women who had built both organizations, the men in the General Conference decided to combine the foreign and home missionary societies, and put them under the control of a male-dominated Board of Missions. One woman missionary was so incensed that

15. Tatum, *Crown of Service,* p. 37.
16. Riley, *Memorial History,* p. 164.
17. Tatum, *Crown of Service,* p. 325.

she resigned from the Methodist church, though she continued her work. As late as 1910 one worried Methodist woman was writing to another that she feared women would "lose their independence of thought when they lost responsibility for, and management of, their own affairs. . . . I fear the future will see the most intelligent women seeking a field of usefulness elsewhere and leave the less intelligent lacking the leadership that leads to enthusiasm and fuller development. . . . We are in a helpless minority in a body where the membership is largely made up of men opposed to independence of thought in women." [18] From long experience the women decided they had no choice but to keep their tempers and try again. Finally in 1918, after repeated rebuffs, Methodist women were granted laity rights.[19] In spite of, perhaps in part because of, the difficulties they encountered, women learned in the churches how to be leaders. As individual women developed purpose and capacity and were frustrated in their plans by unsympathetic males, they came more and more to value independence.

What was called home missionary work was not confined to bringing the gospel to the destitute. In working with poor people, churchwomen encountered many social problems: bad housing, poor food, illiteracy, unemployment, and juvenile delinquency. The social settlement movement, which spread rapidly in the United States after 1890, began in the South on the initiative of Methodist women. In 1882 Miss Laura Haygood organized the Trinity Home Mission in Atlanta, to bring about the "physical, mental and moral

18. Mary Helm to Nellie Nugent Somerville, 29 August 1910, Somerville Papers, Schlesinger Library, Radcliffe College.
19. Tatum, *Crown of Service,* p. 34.

elevation of the poor of the city, and especially of our own Church and congregation." By the end of the first year this society had established an industrial school and a home for dependent and helpless women. From this beginning Methodist women eventually developed a wide network of settlement houses and of welfare work. The Wesley Houses in South Carolina were a response to the needs of mill workers; a community center in Alabama was organized for the Italian workers in the Tennessee Iron and Coal Company; in various towns Methodist women experimented with low-cost boardinghouses for women workers; and some deaconesses undertook missions to the rural population.[20]

The long involvement of southern women with their slaves carried over into a postwar concern for conditions of life in the Negro community. In 1901 the Methodist Woman's Board of Missions took the initiative in adding a girl's industrial training program to the curriculum of Paine College, a Methodist college for Negroes in Augusta, Georgia, and in supplying women for the faculty. In 1911 Miss Mary DeBardelaben of Alabama felt a call to become a missionary to the Negroes and was appointed to work in Augusta, where she organized a Civic Improvement League, a settlement house program, Sunday school, and kindergarten. The Methodist Missionary Council urged women throughout the South to "do all in their power to help and uplift the Negro race." [21]

The direction in which these social concerns took Methodist women became fully apparent in 1916 when the Missionary Council adopted what amounted to a full-scale social gospel program. It included the abolition of child labor,

20. Ibid., pp. 26, 244–45, 268, 295.
21. Ibid., p. 355.

the reduction of illiteracy, prison reform, an end to the convict lease system, the cultivation of "sympathy between all races," and the solution of race problems in a spirit of helpfulness and justice. At their annual meetings the women heard lectures from Jane Addams and Graham Taylor, as well as from southerners who had firsthand experience with industrial conditions in the South.[22]

A strong tradition of social concern had been one of John Wesley's legacies to the Methodist church. That this tradition was still operative in the post–Civil War South is suggested by the leading role of Methodist women's organizations in the developments discussed here as well as by the fact that many of the individual leaders were Methodists.

Not long after church societies began their period of rapid growth they were supplemented by another organization made up solely of women. The Woman's Christian Temperance Union found a sympathetic climate among southern women. Founded in 1874, it had been largely a praying society for the cause of temperance until Frances Willard, a talented young woman who had been head of the Evanston (Illinois) College for Ladies, was made president in 1879. Under her leadership it became one of the most significant women's organizations in the country. In the early eighties Miss Willard made the first of a series of forays into the South. In New Orleans in 1881 she addressed a large audience in the Carondelet Methodist Church. A year later she returned and drafted Caroline Merrick, who had been active in the Methodist missionary society, to be president of the New Orleans WCTU. Mrs. Merrick thought temperance a thankless reform, but she could not refuse the person who, in her view, had done more than any other in the nineteenth

22. Ibid., pp. 350–52.

century to "widen the outlook and develop the mental aspirations" of women.[23] Mrs. Merrick spent ten years as president of the organization, and in that capacity, her contemporaries believed, she was the first woman in Louisiana to
speak in public on public questions.[24]

In 1883 a "few brave souls" summoned a convention of
Christian women in North Carolina and launched the Union
in that state. Six years later in Jackson, Mississippi,
Frances Willard tapped another woman who had not until
that moment know of the existence of the WCTU to become
an organizer. Belle Kearney, the woman in question, felt
after prayerful meditation that she had heard God's call; in
any case she had heard the call of Frances Willard. Miss
Willard's personal effectiveness was one reason the WCTU
spread so rapidly in the South. A southern woman who later
became prominent in national work said, "The first time I
heard her I lay awake all night for sheer gladness. It was
such a wonderful revelation to me that a woman like Miss
Willard could exist. I thanked God and took courage for
humanity." [25]

Many women fastened upon alcohol as the root cause of a
number of related things that bothered them about southern
men and southern life. In their fanatic insistence upon its
eradication, to the point of urging their members to eschew
brandy in puddings, they sometimes made themselves and
their cause ridiculous. But to see them as a joke is to miss
the point.

Drinking had long been a male prerogative and a signifi-

23. Merrick, *Old Times in Dixie Land,* pp. 143–45.
24. Obituary in *New Orleans Times-Picayune,* 30 March 1908.
25. Quoted in Anna A. Gordon, *The Life of Frances Willard* (Evanston, Ill.: National Woman's Christian Temperance Union, 1912), p. 102.

cant part of the life of many southern men. A Georgia woman, editing her Civil War diary for publication in the 1890s, commented in the preface:

In fact, I have been both surprised and shocked in reading over this story of a by-gone generation, to see how prevalent was the use of wines and other alcoholic liquors, and how lightly an occasional over-indulgence was regarded. In this respect there can be no doubt that the world has changed greatly for the better. When "gentlemen" . . . were staying in the house it was a common courtesy to place a bottle of wine, or brandy, or both, with the proper adjuncts, in the room of each guest, so that he might help himself to a "night-cap" on going to bed or an "eye opener" before getting up in the morning.[26]

Miss Andrews's memory of the prewar state of things fitted well with the sentimental fiction of the antebellum years. Novels were filled with husbands discovered to be drunkards by their disillusioned wives only after marriage. In social circles less elevated than that of the Andrews family, the frontiersman's rough-and-ready pleasure in hard drink was well known to the evangelical churches, which early began to preach temperance as necessary to salvation.

The war killed the temperance societies and led to an increase in the drink habit. Observers commented that social drinking and tippling were prevalent everywhere in Reconstruction. The spread of commercial villages and the multiplication of country stores made alcohol more accessible, and its consumption was stimulated by the despondency with which the future was regarded. On Saturday afternoons there were scenes of alcoholic confusion in many

26. Eliza Frances Andrews, *Wartime Journal of a Georgia Girl,* pp. 7–8.

villages.[27] Negroes, whose access to hard drink had been carefully regulated in slavery, joined their white brothers in weekend orgies, though some observers thought them less given to drunkenness than white men. For both races there was a relationship between alcohol and crime, particularly violent crime.

Drinking was therefore troublesome to women for good reason. It led to a threatening social instability and created hardship in many families. The interest of the WCTU in "social purity," a euphemism for control of venereal disease, also represented an attempt to control male behavior. Hopes of putting an end to the double standard in social behavior ran high as women emerged in public life. This goal continued to be a spoken or unspoken part of the platform of women's groups for three decades in the twentieth century.

In antebellum days much had been made by men and women alike of the power of "woman's influence" to bring men, not naturally so inclined, to virtuous habits. But "influence" was a chancy tool at best. The strategy of woman after the Civil War was to work for pledges of total abstinence and statewide prohibition laws, which they hoped would be more effective than influence or persuasion.

The significance of the WCTU went far beyond bringing about prohibition, though it played an important role in doing that. Like the church societies, the WCTU provided a respectable framework in which southern women could pursue their own development and social reform without drastically offending the prevailing views of the community about ladylike behavior. Not many people could seriously object

27. Francis B. Simkins and Robert B. Woody, *Reconstruction in South Carolina* (Chapel Hill: University of North Carolina Press, 1932), pp. 322 ff.

to Christianity and temperance, though one spokesman for the liquor interests told an Atlanta audience that when women left their homes to campaign and work for temperance they forfeited their right to male homage.[28]

As members gained experience the WCTU program expanded. Interest in securing prohibition and anti-alcohol classes in the schools soon took women into politics. The frustration they felt when legislatures listened politely but refused to act turned many WCTU members into suffragists.[29] Still other women, as a result of visiting alcoholics in prison, became prison reformers.

Spurred by Julia Tutwiler in Alabama and Rebecca Latimer Felton in Georgia, the WCTU in the eighties took the lead in fighting the convict lease system in both those states. Mrs. L. C. Blair of Raleigh, North Carolina, told a state legislative committee in 1905 that as superintendent of prison work for the WCTU she had spent ten years studying prisons and the consequences of the way the state dealt with youthful offenders. She begged them to set up a reform school.[30] In Georgia the WCTU headed a movement to establish an industrial school for girls.[31]

The widening interests of the organization were well illustrated in the South Carolina president's speech to the annual convention in that state in 1889. She condemned the convict lease as a "disgrace to the civilization of the nine-

28. Mrs. J. J. Ansley, *History of the Georgia Woman's Christian Temperance Union from 1883 to 1907* (Columbus, Ga., Gilbert Publishing Co., 1914), p. 102.

29. Belle Kearney, *A Slaveholder's Daughter* (New York, 1900), p. 174; see also letters from Madeleine McDowell Breckinridge to WCTU presidents in Kentucky asking them to secure signatures on a suffrage petition, Breckinridge Papers, Library of Congress.

30. *North Carolina White Ribbon* (Charlotte: N.C. W.C.T.U., 1906).

31. Ansley, *History,* p. 119.

teenth century," advocated prenatal care and training for mothers to reduce infant mortality, and called for a reduction in the working hours of labor.

The crusading revivalism of the WCTU appealed to some women frustrated by the churches' ban on women preachers. During an annual convention held in Georgia in 1890 one of the delegates delivered a sermon in the First Baptist Church in Atlanta, and the historian of the organization thought she "brought hundreds of Georgians to recognize the fact that woman could speak in public and not only retain her womanly dignity and graciousness but become in the hands of God a mighty agency for good." [32]

Like the women in the church societies, many WCTU members experienced a personal transformation as they learned to think for themselves, organize programs, and assume leadership. "Southern women have developed marvelously as lecturers and organizers in philanthropic movements," wrote Belle Kearney, who in a more florid moment called the WCTU "the golden key that unlocked the prison doors of pent-up possibilities . . . the discoverer, the developer of southern woman." [33] She herself was an example. In the first year of her "ministry" she traveled all over Mississippi and organized hundreds of unions among young women and children. She held business meetings and discussed the methods of work best suited to forward the interests of the societies she was organizing. In 1889 she went to a national convention in Chicago and gained, she said, " a new vision of woman's life." [34]

Another illustration of the effect of the WCTU upon a

32. Ibid., p. 130.
33. Kearney, *Slaveholder's Daughter*, p. 117.
34. Ibid., pp. 167–68.

talented woman was the case of Mrs. Lide Meriwether of
Memphis, Tennessee, who had been born in 1829. She recorded of herself that after the war she lived a simple home
life, devoted to husband and children. Then, when "most
women are only waiting to die, their children reared and the
tasks of the spirit largely ended, [there] began for her a life
of new thought and activity." A friend in Arkansas asked
her to help at a WCTU convention, where she discovered a
hitherto unknown talent for public speaking. Under her
leadership the Tennessee WCTU grew and flourished, and
from this work she was led into an even more ardent interest
in woman suffrage.[35] Perhaps Frances Willard did not over-
state the case when she referred to her organization, the
largest until that time ever conducted solely by women, as
"a branch of social science and religious activity."[36] She
said that the role of organizer opened a new career to
women. For many southern women this was indeed true.

The biographies of hundreds of women show the same
progression: missionary society, temperance society, woman's club. In the antebellum southern world a woman who
wanted more education than could be found at a local
seminary usually had only her own efforts to fall back on.
By the 1880s, emboldened by their experience in church
societies and the WCTU, inspired by glimpses of activities
in far-off Chicago or New York, stimulated by visits of
famous women from these places, a few southern women
took the bold step of associating themselves in clubs for

35. Willard and Livermore, *American Women* 2: 499.
36. Frances Willard, *Nineteen Beautiful Years* (New York: Fleming
H. Revell, 1889), p. 201.

self-education. Forty years later one of their leaders surveyed the results:

Club experience has been the university in which they have learned [about] themselves and other women and have seen men as one of the species and not as individual husbands and fathers. They have gained respect for their own opinions, toleration for the opinions of others and the necessity of cooperation for the successful accomplishment of all aims. They have discovered the needs and weaknesses of themselves and their homes and have learned how to improve both. Their knowledge has been increased. . . . Gossip has decreased because clubs have given women better things to think about and having seen the needs of the world they have become interested in striving to make their own part of it a little better.[37]

The club movement was national, the beginning almost accidental. It is usually dated from the occasion in 1868 when the New York Press Club, planning a dinner for Charles Dickens, willingly accepted help from their women members in preparing for the dinner but refused to permit them to attend. Jennie June Croly, a talented newspaperwoman, responded to this rejection by gathering a group of other women to whom she suggested that the time had come for them to band together to promote their own interests. None of the women had ever heard of a secular organization composed entirely of women, but Mrs. Croly suggested that there must be many women who had, as she put it, "been seized by the divine spirit of inquiry and aspiration, who were interested in the thought and progress of the age, in what other women were doing." [38]

37. Sallie Southall Cotten, "Accomplishments of Women's Clubs," SSC Papers, 1922, SHC UNC.
38. Mrs. J. C. Croly, *The History of the Woman's Club Movement in America* (New York: H. G. Allen, 1898), pp. 15–16.

Although Mrs. Croly's Sorosis is often mistakenly called the first woman's club, it represented a single case of what was a widespread phenomenon, which spread without any visible proselyting, as if, one woman remarked, by mental telepathy. For example, in 1866 in Quincy, Illinois, a little circle of women calling themselves "Friends in Council" began to meet with the idea of "establishing such a nucleus of thought as would attract and gather about it those who valued the world of thought and were zealous for self-improvement." They spent the winter reading and discussing Lecky's *History of the Rise and Influence of the Spirit of Rationalism in Europe* and Mrs. Child's *Progress of Religious Ideas*.[39] In 1873 the "Light Seekers" were formed in Chicago and heard at their first meeting a paper entitled "Culture for Women." In the next few years many such groups appeared across the country.

Southern women were almost a decade behind the more emancipated eastern and western women. The years 1884–87 were the period when numbers of clubs came spontaneously to life in the South. The initial impulse was often a hunger for education. One of the most ambitious examples of a club which tried to provide a substitute for college was the Atlanta History Club, which, with the help of Herbert Baxter Adams and the encouragement of Daniel Coit Gilman, embarked upon what amounted to a graduate course in nineteenth-century history. The Quid Nunc Club in Little Rock, dissatisfied with "miscellaneous work," spent four years on Greek and Roman history. The spectrum of clubs ranged from these serious ventures through all levels of sophistication, down to a tiny group in Union, South Caro-

39. Ibid., p. 54.

lina, in which the members agreed to read Shakespeare aloud and to correct each other's pronunciation.

The Ladies Literary Club of Spartanburg, South Carolina, drew on another kind of impulse. It was formed in 1884 with the purpose of building a free library for the town. The New Orleans Woman's Club, founded in the same year, was initially attentive to the needs of working women, though it included women from all social classes. Whether educational or civic, these clubs shared some self-consciousness about their pioneering nature. "Club" was still a fearful word to many people, the New Orleans women noted, and in Tennessee one early group called itself the Ossoli Circle, in honor of Margaret Fuller, and said, "In so conservative a city, the idea of a society exclusively for women was novel; organization by women was decidedly an advanced step. Club was not to be thought of and no one dared to propose the name. Friends smiled incredulously, assured that the new fancy would be short-lived." [40]

Straightforward, sometimes naive, southern reports to Mrs. Croly for her giant volume on the history of the woman's club movement said what they thought clubs were all about. "All ages, young and old and middle-aged are gathered in the membership and there is a delightful fraternity of spirit among them," said the Arkansas report. "The old bring their ripe experiences, the young their youth and eager enthusiasm for knowledge. The result is a blending of social and intellectual life as nearly ideal as can be found in this mortal world." In Alabama the "blending" was obvious. The Kettle Drum of Tuscaloosa studied poets and art, and, the reporter remarked, "the refreshments, though

40. Ibid., p. 1077.

simple and limited by law, are always delicious and there is a good deal of rivalry in the making up of dishes." Later in her report she took a more serious view. "Alabama women have begun to discover themselves, their powers, their influence and their responsibilities. They have made a step in advance of self. They are becoming acquainted with conditions as they really exist. They are trying to learn what the hour asks for and have the answer ready." The clubwomen of Georgia called themselves women of "culture and leisure" but said that they were thinking much of "the other woman, in her poverty, ignorance, and hard work." New Orleans women saw themselves as "breaking down and removing barriers of local prejudice . . . assisting the intellectual growth and spiritual ambition in the community." The Nineteenth Century Club of Memphis thought its founders had been "stirred by the modern spirit, and desired ardently to stimulate hope and courage in women, enlarge and increase their intellectual horizon and activities; to better fit them to direct the education and training of their children, and bring them nearer a true place in their husband's life and interests." [41]

In order to understand the hyperbole of these statements it is necessary to remember that women's clubs were then a bold, even a radical departure. Few southern women had access to anything that might reasonably be described as higher education, and there were not many accepted channels—such as organizations or political offices—through which women could work on any problem beyond the domestic walls.

The "duty" and "influence" of the antebellum ideal were

41. All quotations are from Croly, *History,* but were written by various club women.

still operative concepts in women's self-image, but they were extended to a wider world than that of the home. Self-development was most often the original impulse for association, but as every social theorist knows, once a group begins regular association and exchange of ideas there is no telling what the next step will be. In the *Yearbook* of the North Carolina Federation of Women's Clubs for 1912 the president remarked upon the "steady growth and the inevitable development of our women along lines *not dreamed of* in the beginning of our work." [42]

The incredulous friends and skeptical men who thought women's clubs a passing fancy were wrong. They were, instead, an idea whose time had come. Clubs developed rapidly in the South because of a number of prior developments. One antecedent was the soldiers' relief and ladies aid societies during the war which had been transmuted into Confederate memorial associations after the war. These memorial associations represented an early example of organizations of women voluntarily formed for specific goals. The church and temperance societies were even more important, for the courage and self-confidence there developed carried over into club activity in the ensuing decades.

Outside influences also helped to bring clubs into being. Women from other parts of the country came to the South on speaking tours or met their southern counterparts at national conventions of clubs, the WCTU, or suffrage organizations. The importance of Frances Willard's work in stimulating women to action has already been suggested. A Methodist minister in Baton Rouge remarked that "women advocates are springing up in the South and are tolerated

42. Notes in Sallie Southall Cotten Papers, 1912, SHC UNC. Italics mine.

since Miss Willard's tour." [43] The primary result of her efforts was, of course, the mushrooming membership in the WCTU. Equally important was the inspiration she brought and her general invigoration of women in their own behalf. The effect of an encounter with another northern woman—Julia Ward Howe—was dramatically recorded by Belle Kearney: "For many years an earnest desire had possessed me to behold a genuinely strong-minded woman,—one of the truly advanced type. Beautiful to realise she stood before me! and in a position the very acme of independence—upon a platform delivering a speech!" [44]

The development of clubs was also stimulated by various expositions and world's fairs which brought people together and focused attention upon women. As early as 1876 Cornelia Phillips Spencer had noted:

I have been very much interested this past fortnight reading a file of the paper entitled "The New Century for Women," published by a committee of Centennial ladies at the Woman's Pavilion on the Centennial grounds. . . . it may be interesting to learn something of such a publication devoted to the industrial interests of women, noting all the departments of her work at home and abroad, and discussing all means for advancing and improving her opportunities. [45]

A group of Kentucky women reported to Mrs. Croly that "immediately following the Centennial, women's clubs and study classes were organized in various parts of the State." The New Orleans Exposition of 1884 played a similar role in the southwest, and the Columbian Exposition in Chicago

43. Mary Earhart, *Frances Willard: From Prayers to Politics* (Chicago: University of Chicago Press, 1944), p. 180.

44. Belle Kearney, *Slaveholder's Daughter,* p. 108.

45. "The Young Ladies' Column," *North Carolina Presbyterian,* 20 September 1876.

in 1893 was particularly influential in behalf of women. On that occasion each state had a "lady manager," who was responsible, among other things, for her state's display at the exposition. For this purpose the lady manager had first to become well acquainted with her own state, and then with women leaders from all over the country who shared the very active female participation in the fair. A number of the southern lady managers came home with a stronger sense of woman's role in the world than they had ever had before.

Sallie Southall Cotten of North Carolina was one of them. Mrs. Cotten, married in 1865 to a returning Confederate veteran, had spent nearly three decades immersed in busy domesticity. She had seven children, a 2,500-acre plantation, and an active merchant-planter-politician husband. In addition to making pickles, killing hogs, supervising children, and sewing for her large family, she read and thought about woman's place in the world and occasionally wondered whether she had accurately assessed her own personality in choosing to become a wife and mother. When she was forty-seven years old, a family friend and political associate of her husband, Governor Elias Carr, appointed her North Carolina Lady Manager for the Chicago Exposition. The experience transformed her from a woman devoted primarily to home and church into a woman dedicated to the cause of women's clubs. She came back to North Carolina convinced that they were the most hopeful vehicle for progress to be found in the country, and she spent the next twenty years of her life encouraging women to organize, chairing the state federation of women's clubs, and developing her own capacities for leadership. Mrs. Cotten's influence on younger women was one of the formative forces in

North Carolina social history in the first decades of the twentieth century.[46]

Nellie Peters Black, who became a versatile and forceful leader of Georgia women, was already a member of the Atlanta History Club when she was made chairman of hospitals and day nurseries for the Atlanta Exposition of 1895. From this experience grew her lifelong work for free kindergartens for poor children.[47]

The evolution of clubs was, of course, somewhat different in each town and each state, but some general trends were clear. The earliest clubs were almost entirely literary and self-help. They were an answer to a felt need for "culture" or for a degree of education which was rarely available to women in the South in the eighties. While cynics could, with some justice, jibe at the shallowness of the literary and artistic analysis which took place, hardly anybody laughed at what the experience did for the women who participated. As one Arkansas woman wrote, "In thinking of women, her club days and ways, and rejoicing in both, there comes an echo from the past—that clubless past of our grandmothers. Have you ever considered their voiceless condition, and been thankful in your day and generation?"[48]

From literary subjects the women moved rather quickly to social concerns. Even the scholarly Quid Nuncs in Little

46. Sallie Southall Cotten Papers, Biographical Notes, June 1916, SHC UNC. For Mrs. Cotten's influence on others see Hope Summerell Chamberlain, "What's Done and Past," manuscript autobiography, MS Dept., Duke. See also correspondence between Mrs. Cotten and Kate Connor in Henry Groves Connor Papers, SHC UNC, and sketch of SSC in Samuel Ashe et al., *Biographical History of North Carolina* (Greensboro, 1918).

47. Nellie Peters Black Papers, MS Division, University of Georgia Library.

48. Croly, *History*, p. 227.

Rock, with their eyes firmly fixed on Greece and Rome, reported that in order not to be "buried in antiquity" "all the live issues of the day, national, international, social and civic affairs are discussed in connection with the study course." [49] Others began with a civic goal, or moved quickly in that direction. From self-education it was a short step to better education for children. The educational crusade of the nineties and the first decade of the twentieth century drew considerable strength from the women's clubs. [50]

Southern clubwomen undertook a formidable list of civic projects, from planting trees and improving garbage collection in some small towns to the ambitious undertaking of the Rome, Georgia, club, which built a hospital, and the work of the North Carolina Federation of Women's Clubs in helping to build a women's college and to develop university extension courses. [51] Upon the occasion of an annual meeting of the North Carolina Federation a newspaper commented:

The improvement of health, the betterment of morals, the modernizing of education and the humanizing of penology are perhaps the most vital matters of government in which North Carolina women have interested themselves. Any one who can deny either that all these things need improvement or that the activity of the Federated clubs has improved them betrays a startling ignorance of the facts in this state. [52]

These well-bred southern ladies were fearless in choosing subjects for discussion. Perhaps it was partly a result of

49. *Ibid.*, p. 226.
50. A. D. Mayo, "Southern Women in the Recent Educational Movement in the South," *Bureau of Education Circular of Information,* no. 1.
51. Margaret Nell Price, "The Development of Leadership by Southern Women through Clubs and Organizations," master's thesis, University of North Carolina, 1945.
52. *The Southerner,* 28 January 1912, clipping in Sallie Southall Cotten Scrapbook, SHC UNC.

naiveté that in the first decades they boldly attacked problems from child labor and sweatshops to "fallen women," a category of whose existence proper southern ladies were supposed to be ignorant. Since most of the reporting of club activities took place in the woman's pages of newspapers or in their own publications, perhaps many men simply did not know, and the women wisely did not tell them, what was going on.

Even a book club might be a source of dangerous ideas. A North Carolina woman spoke of hers:

Ibsen was the first of the newer prophets to fall into our hands. Imagine the intoxication of the thing! thereafter we read Shaw, and Ellen Key and made a headlong leap into the literature of feminism and suffrage agitation then beginning to stir. . . . Our little circle lived on with a few changes of personnel for at least ten years and always it was a center of stimulation and formative interest in my life.[53]

One social concern led to another, and the social concerns inevitably led to politics. Women who once had barely been able to chair a meeting made up of close friends found themselves at work in the halls of the legislature. One of them remarked:

Our new experience of speaking with legislators had broadened our perspective and taught us not the least important an education of ourselves. . . . so step by step we have grown and gradually our conception of woman's sphere has enlarged, and we realise that the average legislator is open to the force of logic and facts.[54]

53. Hope Summerell Chamberlain, "What's Done and Past," pp. 71–72.

54. Library Extension Report, North Carolina Federation of Women's Clubs, May 1909, in Sallie Southall Cotten Papers, SHC UNC.

Women gradually came to recognize the strength inherent in combined forces. Between 1894 (Kentucky) and 1907 (Virginia) federations of clubs were formed in every southern state. By 1910 all these federations had been admitted to the General Federation of Women's Clubs. In union there was strength. Perhaps even more important was the stimulating effect of exchanging ideas, another example of the tendency of association to carry people beyond their original goals. The federations developed into agencies for building public opinion and dramatizing the needs of the state.

The role of the General Federation of Women's Clubs as an inspirer of southern women was plainly illustrated in a report to Agnes Morris, a dedicated clubwoman of Natchitoches, Louisiana, from a woman who had been a delegate to the Fifth Biennial Convention in Milwaukee. The delegate noted, and reported to her Louisiana constituents, "a fast growing spirit of altruism among club members." Instead of literary culture, women were becoming interested in town libraries. Instead of teaching themselves about art, they were giving attention to public school decoration and to art in their towns. Musical clubs were bringing good music to the public. The key woman, she observed, was "she who strives for the solution of the questions of wage-earning women, of the underage working children, of the Consumers League, of the Sanitation Clubs, of the political equality movement." At Milwaukee she had heard an Atlanta woman talk of the need for work among Negro children and was introduced to the concept of the Consumers League and its fight against sweatshops. In conclusion the delegate congratulated her local club upon being a factor in a group "so tremendous in size and influence, and would hope that it may ever give of the richness of its life to help in the forward movement of this united sisterhood." [55]

Clubs also became a training school for women who wanted to serve in public life. As officials of state governments came gradually to accept the idea that women might contribute something to the leadership of public institutions it was to the ranks of clubwomen that they turned to seek individuals who might be appointed to office. In North Carolina clubwomen worked hard to expand the state's responsibility for public welfare and were rewarded by seeing one of their number made welfare commissioner. Another was put on the board of the state training school for boys, after women had worked for its establishment. Some women who had joined organizations in the first instance to pursue social or personal development found that the competence gained through club experience opened new doors. For those with real ambition clubs and women's groups were one of the few available roads to anything approaching real power. [56] There was nothing uniquely feminine about combining personal ambition with public service, but the opportunity for women to do so was a new thing in the postwar South.

In 1913 Mrs. Cotten of North Carolina tried to sum up the whole matter:

Never until today has educated, Christianized woman come into consciousness of her power and responsibility. Never until today have her activities extended beyond the limits of her own household. Today the world is calling her and she is responding, sometimes against her own inclination, often against the

55. Agnes Morris Papers, Report on Miluaukee Convention, Dept. of Archives, LSU.

56. See again Price, "The Development of Leadership."

wishes of man, but the summons is imperative—she must obey. The welfare of future generations calls to her.[57]

In the same year a dean of the University of North Carolina attributed much the same significance to clubs:

Women's clubs, by following the line of service to the home, have discovered a field of service to the state that has sent a current of intellectual interest and civic achievement not only through the life of women unequalled by any other force, but through that of men as well. There is no greater stimulus to that right reason that is the aim of higher education than the responsibility of making it prevail.[58]

The power of association had its own inner dynamic, which carried many women to points they had not, in the beginning, been able to envision.

57. Sallie Southall Cotten Scrapbook, Reports of the 1913 Convention of the N.C. General Federation of Women's Clubs, SHC UNC.
58. Edward Kidder Graham, dean of the College of Liberal Arts, UNC, to the 10th annual meeting of the Southern Association of College Women, Richmond, Va., April 1913, in *Proceedings of the Tenth Annual Meeting.*

. . . no race of men can rise
above their mothers. The suffrage
movement is an effort to elevate
the entire race by elevating its
womanhood.

Nellie Nugent Sommerville,
president of the Mississippi
Suffrage Association

7

The Right to Vote

S he wants the vote to use as a lever, and so do I," said the heroine of a Virginia novel, "but behind it all . . . I am fighting for plain recognition of an equal humanity." [1] Thus she summed up the two sides of the suffrage movement. Suffrage came to symbolize feminism in the widest sense, the desire of women to break out of their narrow sphere and establish themselves as independent beings. Women also wanted the vote for practical reasons. As they moved out of their homes to take jobs where they were paid less than men, or into organizations where they hoped to achieve social goals by legislation, the need for the vote was increasingly felt. The symbolic meaning was constantly juxtaposed with the practical.

A Kentucky suffragist wrote, "There are many women in the South gifted with genius and endowed with faculties for glorious work, who are struggling to free themselves from the austerity of those environments which 'the masses of average men' have fixed for them." To this sweeping justification for suffrage she immediately added a list of practical objectives which women wanted and thought they could secure only by voting: admission to state universities, the building of industrial training schools, improvements in taxation, and the like. She appended statements from seventy women, each giving her reasons for being a suffragist. Those too were divided between the general and the specific. Some spoke of "simple justice," the need for women to have serious subjects for thought, the danger that any disfranchised class would be servile and subject, the demoralizing nature of influence without responsibility. Others listed such concrete goals as changes in the age-of-consent laws, better

1. Mary Johnston, *Hagar* (Boston: Houghton Mifflin, 1913), p. 331.

schools, and control of venereal disease.[2] The heroine of a
Tennessee suffragist novel "longed to be free, to be wild as
the creatures that roamed the mountain tops." A few pages
later she spoke of "average men who take it for granted that
a woman was made for a servant, and that in administering
to the wants of her household she fulfilled her earthly
mission."[3] The president of the Virginia Equal Suffrage
League offered her followers the argument that women
could never fully develop their capabilities as long as they
remained "under guardianship" and were deprived of the
education which the practice of self-government provided.[4]
A Georgia leader offered a similar rationale: "The call of the
age is for partnership in the family, in the church, in the
State and National affairs, between men and women."[5]
Suffrage more than any other aspect of the feminist movement became the symbol of women's emancipation. Partly
this was because, historically, voting had been associated
with the idea of equal rights, partly because it was a general
goal upon which women with many different specific pur-
poses could agree.

To its opponents as well, "woman suffrage" meant more
than women voting. In itself the idea that women might join
the electorate was hardly revolutionary; the thrust of the
nineteenth century had been toward a broader franchise.
But for every suffragist who linked the vote to her human-

2. *The Arena* February 1895, p. 354.

3. Hannah J. Price, *The Closed Door* (Knoxville: Knoxville Litho-
graphing Co., 1913), pp. 30, 32.

4. Lila Meade Valentine, quoted in *History of Woman Suffrage,* ed.
Ida Husted Harper, 5 (New York, 1922): 492–93.

5. Rebecca Latimer Felton, "On the Subjection and Enfranchisement
of Women," pamphlet in the R. L. Felton Papers, MS Division, University of Georgia Library.

ity, there were men (and also women) who equated ballots for females with a terrifying threat to society.

Senator Joseph Brown of Georgia summed up the case for the opposition in a speech before the Senate in 1887. God, the senator asserted, had intended the sexes to be different. Their duties and obligations were of equal value but they could never be the same. Man was created to be head of the family and deal with "the sterner realities and difficulties." It was up to men to take responsibility for the state, in military and political matters. Politics was in its nature laborious and for its practice "the male sex is infinitely better suited than the female." Woman was formed for other things. Brown continued:

In the family she is *queen*. She alone is fitted for the discharge of the sacred trust of wife and the endearing relation of mother. While the man is contending with the sterner duties of life, the *whole time* of the noble, affectionate and true woman is required in the discharge of the delicate and difficult duties assigned her in the family circle, in her church relations and in the society where her lot is cast.

Because the duties of motherhood were vital, Brown contended, society would be unwise to burden women with others which were, in any case, beyond their strength. Women had plenty of influence without the vote. Were suffrage granted, only the "baser class" of women would go to the polls; refined ladies would stay at home.

Brown recognized the argument that single women had no man to represent them. His response was to warn Congress not to do anything which might encourage women to remain single. To clinch this argument, he asserted that the largest number of divorces were found in communities with the largest number of advocates of female suffrage—where, as he put it, "the individuality of woman as related to her husband, which such a doctrine inculcates, is increased to the greatest extent." [6]

More than forty years of debate on woman suffrage lay ahead when Senator Brown spoke. His speech encompassed most of the arguments upon which southern politicians were to rely during those years. There had only to be added the warning that enfranchisement of women would bring Negro women into the electorate, and the blueprint for the opposition ideology was complete. [7]

The opposition drew heavily on the "queen of the home" tradition, and Senator Brown's speech echoed a thousand antebellum apotheoses of women. It suggested a depth of fear reminiscent of George Fitzhugh's frantic strictures in the fifties. Many of the men who were so eloquent in opposition to suffrage *were* fearful of changing the desirable state of affairs in the "man's world" in which they had grown up. The Negro slaves had been emancipated but women were still providing men with creature comforts and bolstering their egos.

6. Susan B. Anthony and Ida H. Harper, eds., *History of Woman Suffrage* 4 (Rochester, 1902): 93–104. The women who edited the *History* could not resist taking a few pot shots at Brown in their footnotes; so when he argued that enfranchisement carried with it the responsibility of jury service and military duty, activities unsuitable for women, they noted that as a lawyer he was exempt from the first, and that he had also managed to avoid going into uniform during the Civil War.

7. In 1914 after the first effort to secure a state suffrage amendment in Mississippi had failed, the president of the suffrage association summed up the arguments most frequently met. "Besides the negro question, First, Biblical—that women suffrage is contrary to the scripture. Second —Mississippi women are taken care of and do not need the ballot and third that we do not have a sufficient showing of support." Nellie Nugent Somerville Papers, Schlesinger Library, Radcliffe College.

In 1909 one Robert Holland, perhaps a college professor, summed up male fears in an article in the *Sewanee Review*. Society forbade suffrage to women, Holland asserted, "having as jealous an eye to the honor of women as to the strength of men in its contemplation of the supreme welfare of the community." Female honor, he argued, was incompatible with voting. "Her finer being has thus far refined Society by keeping out of its turmoil." Unless the unseemly demand for "rights" ceased, he predicted, women would gradually grow ugly and coarse. Strife would characterize family life, and in the end there would be utter disaster, since "the first principle of religion is obedience. The woman who does not obey her husband will not obey God who enjoins her submission." [8]

Men were not alone in opposing suffrage in the South. Substantial numbers of southern women were slow to see any advantage to themselves and were afraid to believe in something which displeased men. "We do not need the ballot in Louisiana to protect any of our just rights and privileges," wrote one woman. "Every Southern woman has a protection and champion in every Southern man." Two decades later another wrote that southern women did not want the vote because they wanted "to preserve in their daughters the salient characteristics of a past generation." Giving women the vote, she said, would lead to divisions and dissensions in the home, hitherto "the source of all good in the state." The glory of womanhood had been "her purity, her superiority to man in the possession of a higher moral sense and standard. Why risk this precious certainty

8. Robert Afton Holland, "The Suffragette," *Sewanee Review* 17 (July 1909): 278–88.

for a doubtful good?"[9] The antisuffrage arguments drew heavily on the old image of southern woman in danger of becoming unfeminine if she dared to step out of her natural sphere.

The South was slow to develop an organized suffrage movement. In 1848 the women who met at Seneca Falls had included the right to vote in their list of demands. Because many of the early suffragists were abolitionists, the idea of woman's rights was anathema in the South. An antebellum woman who felt sympathy with the Seneca Falls Declaration did not say so out loud. In 1913 an ancient lady in Hillsboro, North Carolina, announced herself to be the oldest suffragist in the state—but she had waited sixty-odd years to make the fact public. Like Elizabeth Cady Stanton, she was a lawyer's daughter whose observations of her father's practice had convinced her that the law was unjust to women. Unlike Mrs. Stanton, however, she did not make her private conviction the basis for a public movement.[10]

That there were secret suffragists scattered about the South became apparent immediately after the war as certain individual southern women suddenly appeared as active members of the national woman's rights movement. In 1867 a Kentucky woman was a vice-president of the Equal Rights Association, and a year or two later a contingent of

9. *New Orleans Daily Item,* 5 July 1879; Annah Robinson Watson, "The Attitude of Southern Women on the Suffrage Question," *The Arena,* February 1895, pp. 363–69.

10. The woman's name was Sarah Jane Bailey, and the occasion for her belated announcement was the election of her grandson's wife to the presidency of the Equal Suffrage League of North Carolina. Clipping from the *Raleigh News and Observer,* undated but apparently from 1913, in John Steele Henderson Papers, SHC UNC.

southern women attended the national convention of the association. By 1869 women from Virginia, North Carolina, South Carolina, Texas, Florida, and Tennessee were listed as vice-presidents. In 1870 Paulina Wright Davis, a northern suffragist visiting in Richmond, discovered there a woman who was "a most earnest advocate of the ballot for women." Together they enlisted the interest of other Richmond women, and with the help of Matilda Joslyn Gage of Ohio organized a Virginia Suffrage Association, which included a number of men. The Virginia woman, Mrs. Bodeker, tried to vote in 1871, and when she failed, deposited in the ballot box a paper asserting her right to do so.[11] By 1873 Elizabeth Avery Meriwether of Tennessee and Priscilla Holmes Drake of Alabama were speaking at the national suffrage convention.

During the presidential campaign of 1868 a Georgia woman reflected in her diary:

I do not in my heart wonder that the Negroes vote the Radical ticket, and to have persuaded them otherwise would be against my own conscience. Think of the right to vote, that right which they have seen their old masters exercise with so much pride, and their young masters look forward to with so much pleasure is *within their grasp.* They secure a right for themselves which it is true they may not understand, but they have children whom they expect to educate, shall they secure this right for them, or sell their right away? It is within their grasp, who can guarantee that they will ever have it extended to them again?

If the women of the North once secured to me the right to vote whilst it might be an honor thrust upon me I think I should think twice before I voted to have it taken from me. Of

11. Elizabeth Cady Stanton et al., eds., *History of Woman Suffrage* 2 (New York, 1882): 345; 3 (New York, 1886): 823–24.

course such sentiments smack too much of radicalism to promulgate outside my own family.[12]

Signs of suffrage sentiment appeared here and there in the South in the first decade after the war. In 1869 suffrage resolutions were presented to constitutional conventions in Texas and Arkansas. A woman's rights convention was held in Columbia, South Carolina, in 1870 with the blessing of the Reconstruction government. The chairman, Miss L. M. Rollin, had supporting letters from such leading Republicans as Governor Scott and D. H. Chamberlain. In 1876 a Mississippi woman addressed the Democratic Convention, assembled in Nashville, in behalf of woman suffrage.[13]

By the 1870s Cornelia Phillips Spencer's sensitive antennae picked up the new signals.

I confess to being so blind and bigoted that only lately has it occurred to me that there might be some good on the other side of Woman's Rights. Only lately have I looked at it dispassionately and find to my inexpressible surprise and disgust that the female reformers out yonder in Wyoming, Chicago, New York and whatnot, except down South, really have an argument or two on their side.[14]

In 1872 an avowed champion of woman's rights stood for Congress in the Fifth District of Alabama. In the same year Hannah Tracy Cutler and Margaret V. Longley were granted a "respectful hearing" on the subject of suffrage from the Kentucky legislature.

These flurries of suffrage sentiment did not represent a

12. Diary of E. G. C. Thomas, October 1868, MS Dept., Duke.
13. Elizabeth Taylor, *Woman Suffrage Movement in Tennessee* (New York: Bookman Associates, 1959), p. 15.
14. "The Young Ladies' Column," *North Carolina Presbyterian,* 5 January 1870.

large body of opinion. A report from Alabama in the third volume of the *History of Woman Suffrage,* published in 1886, noted that women there were "awake on the temperance question" but unprepared for suffrage. As late as 1897 a national organizer traveling in Mississippi wrote bitterly that suffrage was often seen as a "heresy that has a real devil in it," and that "death and education have much to do in this southland." [15]

Through the seventies and eighties, however, a few indefatigable women kept the fires alive. In Kentucky the four Clay sisters—Mary, Anne, Sallie, and Laura—were virtually a suffrage organization in themselves. In Tennessee, Elizabeth Avery Meriwether, described as "the chief representative of liberal thought in Tennessee," was a hardy soul who had survived a difficult period as a war refugee and had come back to Memphis after the war to establish and edit her own newspaper, called *The Tablet.* Years later her son said that shortly after the war when her husband was engaged in organizing a local Ku Klux Klan, Mrs. Meriwether had suggested giving the vote to white women as an alternative to terrorizing Negro men. In November 1876 she applied for the privilege of voting in the presidential election and rented a Memphis theater to explain her reasons to all who cared to listen. The hall filled pretty well, she said, since her lecture was free! By 1881 she was traveling the suffrage circuit in New England and drawing praise from the *Boston Herald* for her wit and charm. Encouraged by this New England success to try a tour in Arkansas and Texas, she found "unreasoning prejudice" so strong that she resorted to speaking on temperance instead. In Sherman,

15. Ella Harrison to Carrie Chapman Catt, 18 and 27 March 1897, Ella Harrison Papers, Schlesinger Library, Radcliffe College.

Texas, the newspaper conceded that her manner was that of a refined and cultivated southern lady, and "as such we respect her enthusiastic advocacy of a cause, Eutopian [*sic*] though it be." [16]

Mrs. Meriwether had a friend and counterpart in Louisiana, another strong-minded woman named Elizabeth Lyle Saxon. Mrs. Saxon was born in Tennessee in the 1830s, had gone for a while to the school of the novelist Caroline Lee Hentz, who may have started her thinking about the trials of a woman's life, and at sixteen married an Alabama Unionist. She had seven children, spent part of the war period in New York, and turned up in New Orleans soon thereafter. For the next thirty years she was active in many kinds of reform movements connected with women and wrote for a number of newspapers on the subjects of her interest. In 1879 she secured five hundred signatures to a woman suffrage petition which she laid before the Louisiana Constitutional Convention. Her coadjutor in this venture was Caroline Merrick, whose interest in suffrage was also of prewar origin. She, too, had been a bright, precocious girl who married at fifteen (which meant, she noted, that she was essentially "brought up" by her lawyer husband who was considerably older). "I early ascertained," she wrote in her memoirs, "that girls had a sphere wherein they were expected to remain and that the despotic hand of some man was continually lifted to keep them revolving in a certain

16. Elizabeth Avery Meriwether, *Recollections of 92 Years* (Nashville, 1958), passim. The historian is rightly trained to suspect memoirs, especially those which look to the distant past. However, some of Mrs. Meriwether's recollections are corroborated by contemporary documents in the *History of Woman Suffrage*. Furthermore, the benefit of any doubt must certainly be given to a woman who could write so lively and coherent a volume at the age of ninety-two.

prescribed and very restricted orbit." [17] In 1879 she was grieving for a beloved daughter, a victim of the great yellow fever epidemic of 1878; Mrs. Saxon urged her to assuage her grief by trying to do something for women who were still alive. Encouraged by her husband, she agreed, and wrote a cogent speech. When the moment for delivery came, she nearly lost courage and was on the point of asking her son-in-law to read the speech when Mrs. Saxon reminded her that they were there to object to being represented by men. So she read her own speech. She later said the surprise could hardly have been greater if, twenty-five years earlier, a procession of slaves had appeared at the big house to ask for their freedom. The *Daily Picayune* spoke kindly of her talk, and one member of the convention was moved to offer a resolution in favor of woman suffrage.

There were others—women born in the thirties and forties, raised in the antebellum culture but prepared now to shake off many of its presuppositions. The ideological commitment of these women was varied, but each in her own way was a remarkably strong person. Their own abilities and performance cast doubt on the shibboleths about woman's inferiority, or her inability to perform hard jobs. Laura Clay wrote in her diary in 1864: "I am a woman, but I think I have a mind superior to that of many boys of my age, and equal to that of many more. Therefore when we get to heaven we will be equal." Ten years later she noted in the same journal that God had called her to the great cause of woman's rights.[18]

Belle Kearney, who went from temperance to suffrage work in Mississippi, hinted at part of her own motivation

17. *Old Times in Dixie Land,* p. 12.
18. Diary, Laura Clay Papers, 15 May 1864, University of Kentucky.

when she wrote, "Of all unhappy sights the most pitiable is that of a human life, rich in possibilities and strong with divine yearnings for better things than it has known, atrophying in the prison house of blind and palsied custom," [19] and later added, "Since the development of my reasoning faculties I had believed in the rights of women. . . . There was born in me a sense of the injustice that had always been heaped upon my sex, and this consciousness created and sustained in me a constant and ever increasing rebellion." [20]

These early suffragists did not need a "movement" to bring them to the cause. Two things they had in common: a strong sense of their own capacities and the ability to be self-starting. Some of them had begun to show maverick tendencies before the war. Those who were old enough had faced the war itself with independence and courage and afterward were prepared for the ridicule and scorn often directed at "strong-minded" women. Indeed, some of them seemed to gain positive satisfaction from being different; involvement in the suffrage struggle gave them an independence and an identity which they found much to their taste.

It was a long jump from the bold individual assertions of a handful of women to an organized suffrage movement. Such a movement could not come into being until there were followers as well as leaders, until the church societies, the WCTU, and the clubs had created a potential constituency of self-confident women, until a considerable number of working women began to feel the vulnerability of their voteless state, and until a number of highly respected men were ready to endorse the goal.

19. *A Slaveholder's Daughter,* p. 41.
20. Ibid., p. 108.

By the mid-nineties these conditions had come into being. A generation of women born since the war was arriving at maturity, the number of working women was steadily increasing, and communication with the world outside the South was ever more active. In 1896 five southern women were among the nineteen who testified at length before the Senate Committee on Woman Suffrage, and by that year some degree of suffrage organization had taken place in every southern state.[21] In every state a few prominent men were openly supporting women's right to vote.

The change which was beginning to take place in the South was clear on every page of the southern state reports included in the fourth volume of the *History of Woman Suffrage,* published in 1902, covering the years 1883 to 1900. The Alabama reporter, for example, noted that "the strength of the woman movement in the State has wonderfully developed in the last five years." Similar statements were made about other southern states. In Arkansas a newspaper especially devoted to the interests of women and strongly advocating suffrage was said to be having an effect. The national suffrage convention had been held in Georgia in 1895, and a new wave of interest had followed.[22]

Suffrage organizations did not limit themselves to the single cause of the ballot. The New Orleans Equal Rights Association, for example, took the lead first in the anti-lottry campaign and then in securing modern sewage and

21. Margaret Nell Price, "The Development of Leadership by Southern Women through Clubs and Organizations," master's thesis, University of North Carolina, 1945, contains an excellent summary of the progress of southern suffrage organization, and charts the dates at which interest began in each state, the dates of the first statewide associations, and periods when interest seemed to lapse.

22. *History of Woman Suffrage* 4: 465 ff.

drainage and a pure water supply. Dramatic success in both ventures made new converts to the suffrage cause. Conversely, when women became interested in temperance or child labor and found themselves spurned by legislators, the drive for suffrage gained a new impetus. "After seeing the defeat of a constitutional amendment for prohibition despite the earnest but ineffectual efforts of the women who besieged the polls," Miss Mary Partridge of Alabama decided the time had come to do something about suffrage. In the ensuing seven years she helped organize eighty-seven suffrage groups and converted, so she thought, thirty-two newspaper editors along the way. After a hard battle in the Louisiana legislature over a child labor bill, Jean Gordon noted that the theory that wives could influence their husbands had been totally disproved, since every member who voted against the bill had a wife who favored it, and "in that moment was sown the seeds of a belief in the potency of the ballot beyond that of woman's influence." [23]

The record shows southern suffragists to have been engaged in a wide variety of reform efforts. In addition to their concern for temperance, child labor, and the working conditions of women, suffrage groups worked for women's colleges, for laws which would permit women to serve on school boards, for tuberculosis control, for prenatal clinics, and for modification in the age of consent. In 1915 the Woman Suffrage party of Louisiana persuaded the Men's League for Woman Suffrage to set up an organization of women taxpayers to which all women property owners in

23. Merrick, *Old Times,* p. 218, on the significance of the women's anti-lottery campaign; *History of Woman Suffrage* 5: 312; Jean Gordon, "New Louisiana Child Labor law," *Charities* 21 (26 January 1903): 481.

the state would be eligible, to study the taxation, assessment, and financial problems of the state, parish, and city, and "to take such action as might be necessary to secure good government, justice, economy and efficiency." By bringing women's efforts to bear on concrete issues the Suffrage party was following the pattern which astute leaders had used all along to broaden their base of support.[24]

After 1910 suffragists multiplied and new suffrage organizations appeared in many places. Alabama, which had two suffrage groups in 1910 had eighty-one by 1917. North Carolina reported a tenfold membership increase in the single year 1917. Men's leagues for woman suffrage were organized, and college suffrage leagues became fashionable. More and more newspapers moved into the suffrage column, and suffrage meetings began to be held in such respectable places as governors' mansions and Senate chambers.

As early as 1909 Professor Holland in his bitter article in the *Sewanee Review* had complained: "The platform fustian about woman's enslavement to man, the wrong she has suffered at man's hands, the time-long stunting of her faculties by man's repression, has been iterated until many quiet women are beginning to believe it with a smoldering resentment at their misfortune at man's infliction." Whereas it had once required great courage to be a suffrage supporter, a subtle change was underway, and, Holland said, "no man may criticize the Woman's Movement without danger to his ears."[25]

Growth in respectability changed the nature of the move-

24. Ethel Hutson to W. A. Kernaghan, 18 August 1915, Ethel Hutson Papers, Ms. Dept., Tulane University. See also Nellie Nugent Somerville, notes for history of Women Suffrage Movement in Mississippi, Somerville-Howorth Papers, Schlesinger Library, Radcliffe.

25. Robert Holland, "The Suffragette," p. 273.

ment. No longer was every suffragist necessarily a bold and dedicated soul. By 1915 there was enough psychological support to reassure the timorous, and the composition of suffrage organizations changed accordingly. With enough support, some of the mice became lions.

The change in atmosphere was again reflected in the sixth volume of the *History of Woman Suffrage,* published after the Ninetenth Amendment was adopted but covering the years immediately before. Influential ministers had begun to speak out from the pulpit; vast quantities of printed matter were circulated. By 1916 the United Daughters of the Confederacy and the Daughters of the American Revolution were openly working for suffrage in Mississippi. Respectability could go no further. The bandwagon was rolling. The southern suffrage movement became a full-scale political campaign, with an array of gifted orators, petitions, hearings, national meetings, and propaganda agencies. The rush of politicians to what now appeared to be the winning side was noted with satisfaction and mild cynicism by women who had been in the movement for decades.

Through all the time from the early nineties until the accomplishment of suffrage in 1920 the southern movement had certain strongly marked regional characteristics. The power of ancient patterns persisted. Women were always reminding each other of the importance of being ladylike. "An unpleasant aggressiveness will doubtless be expected of us," a Mississippi leader once warned; "let us endeavor to disappoint such expectations." [26] North Carolina suffragists went on record in 1914 as opposing "any form of militancy"

26. Nellie Nugent Somerville, notes, 1898, Somerville-Howorth Papers, Schlesinger Library, Radcliffe College.

and "desiring to gain the vote by an appeal to reason and fair play." [27] A Virginia leader remarked that "the wise suffrage leaders here have realised . . . that success depends upon showing their cause to be compatible with the essentials of the Virginia tradition of womanliness." [28] Directions from officers to local groups of suffrage women were filled with injunctions to be tactful. Newspaper reports tended to emphasize the beauty and femininity of suffrage leaders. Judith Hyams Douglas, a woman lawyer and active suffrage leader in Louisiana, once described the members of the famous New Orleans ERA club as "physicians, dentists, journalists, attorneys, philanthropists," all presenting "a very feminine appearance," and she emphasized that women could be interested in the affairs of the country "without looking or desiring to be in the least like a man." [29] Because the environment was often hostile, southern suffrage groups were more dependent than those in the North or West upon a few strong, gifted leaders and less upon large numbers of followers. The suffrage movement everywhere provided an opportunity for strong women to become stronger, and for personalities to develop. This was particularly true in the South.

The race question also gave a regional coloring to the southern suffrage movement. On the one hand, anti-suffrage southerners never wearied of arguing that giving votes to women would bring black women into the electorate. To this suffrage leaders rejoined, in the words of one of them, "As our men in Georgia have paddled down the voting

27. Elizabeth Taylor, "Woman Suffrage Movement in North Carolina," *North Carolina Historical Review* 38 (April 1961): 176.
28. Orie Lathan Hatcher, "The Virginia Man and the New Era for Women," *Nation* 106 (1 June 1918): 560–62.
29. Clipping, Judith Hyams Douglas Papers, Dept. of Archives, LSU.

stream for nearly a half century, with negro men cooks and barbers, etc. we will not cross that bridge before we come to it." [30]

On the other hand, a recent student of the ideas of the woman suffrage movement has observed that some southern women talked as if their primary concern was to counterbalance the Negro vote by that of "educated, cultivated women without resorting to means of doubtful constitutionality," such as the grandfather clause, the white primary, and the like.[31] Some southern leaders did, indeed, argue their case in these terms. Belle Kearney, for example, once told a national suffrage convention that "the South [will] be compelled to look to its Anglo-Saxon women as the medium through which to retain the supremacy of the white race over the African." She added that few people recognized this obvious fact, including, presumably, few of her colleagues in the suffrage movement.[32]

Such arguments were a part, though a minor one, of a complicated mixture of real motives and political arguments which southern women developed. In 1895 five hundred-odd Tennessee women issued an eleven-point Confession of Faith, of which the eleventh point was, "We educated women want the power to offset the illiterate vote of our State." The other ten points had to do with the right of taxpayers to representation, the need for improvement in the legal status of women, women's right to keep their earnings, and so on. Another familiar argument was exem-

30. Rebecca Latimer Felton, "On the Subjection and Enfranchisement of Women," pamphlet in the William Felton Papers, University of Georgia.

31. Aileen Kraditor, *Ideas of the Woman Suffrage Movement* (New York: Columbia University Press, 1965), p. 173.

32. *History of Woman Suffrage* 5: 83.

plified in 1911 when Arkansas women told the house committee on constitutional amendments of their state legislature that they needed the ballot in order to achieve pure food laws, street cleaning departments, an end to the tenement evil, and other vital municipal reforms, adding that it was "uneconomical, inefficient and unsatisfactory to endeavor to secure these needed reforms through husbands and brothers." [33] Southern women, like suffrage supporters elsewhere, had a large repertory of arguments, and they were careful to use the ones they thought most effective for the audience at hand.

The regional cast to the suffrage movement was also visible in Washington. Maud Wood Park, a New England woman who was in charge of the last phase of the congressional campaign, recorded her observations of the southern members of her committee. Of one she wrote:

33. Sue Shelton White Papers, Schlesinger Library, Radcliffe College; *Arkansas Gazette,* 16 March 1911, quoted by Elizabeth Taylor in *Arkansas Historical Quarterly,* Spring 1956, p. 15. Insight into the racial views prevalent in the South in 1900 may be gained from Katherine DuPre Lumpkin, *The Making of a Southerner* (New York: Knopf, 1947), especially the chapter "A Child Inherits the Lost Cause." See also Ray Stannard Baker, *Following the Color Line* (New York: Doubleday, Page, 1908). Both Aileen Kraditor, in the work cited (n. 31 above), and Alan Grimes have recently raised a question whether the drive for woman suffrage was essentially a conservative movement, aimed at counteracting the disruptive effects of immigrant and Negro voters. That the desire for social stability was one motive among women in the suffrage movement is beyond question, but to define the movement therefore as "conservative" is to use the word in a very special sense. In the South especially, a woman was generally viewed as extremely radical once she openly espoused suffrage. It is beyond any doubt that southern women wanted the vote primarily because of their concern about the place of women in the world, not because of their concern about the place of Negroes.

But the thing about her which took my breath away was her complimentary attitude with the southern members. It was so extreme that I feared the men to whom it was addressed would think we had deliberately sent a honey-tongued charmer . . . to cajole them. . . . Something of this I felt constrained to hint to our chairman, who replied . . . that southern men were so accustomed to that sort of persiflage they would think a woman unfeminine if she failed to use it.[34]

She added that the southern women were the most charming of her cadre of lobbyists, and were invited so often to lunch with their senators that she began to fear some compromise of the cause.[35]

Despite its significance in training numbers of women in politics, despite the symbolism that it developed for women in search of a new life-style, the organized effort to attain woman suffrage was less effective in the South than in almost any other part of the country. When the Nineteenth Amendment passed the Congress and was sent to the states for ratification, only Texas, Tennessee, Kentucky, and Arkansas among southern states voted to accept it. Women mounted vigorous campaigns in all the other states, but were defeated. They wasted little time in regret. They accepted suffrage as a gift from fellow citizens outside the South and went promptly to work to give meaning to the new-found right.

34. *Front Door Lobby,* ed. Edna Lamprey Stantial (Boston: Beacon Press, 1960), p. 27.
35. Ibid., p. 43.

It is striking to note how quickly
the women of some of the
southern and southwestern states
are growing active and even
influential. If they will but exert
a good and beneficent influence
in politics and public affairs,
feminism in politics may prove
a great blessing to the country.

Danville (Va.) *Register*,
6 August 1922

8

Women with the Vote

Women had been saying for years that the world, and they themselves, would be changed if they were granted the right to vote. When Tennessee ratified the Nineteenth Amendment, the old dream became reality. Would the predicted consequences follow?

For more than two decades increasing numbers of southern women had become deeply engaged in efforts to build a system of public schools, to clean up prisons and abolish the convict lease system, to restrict the use of child labor, to improve the working conditions and reduce the hours of work of women and of factory workers generally, and to diminish racial discrimination in the South. Progress in all these areas had been slow, and the World War diverted the energies of many reformers. Now the war was over, women had the ballot, and the time had come when it was possible to believe, as one young North Carolina woman put it, that "the advent of women into political life would mean the loosening of a great moral force which will modify and soften the relentlessly selfish economic forces of trade and industry. . . . the ideals of democracy and of social and human welfare will undoubtedly receive a great impetus." [1]

Whatever the future was destined to reveal about the long-run consequences of adding women to the electorate, at the outset there was a burst of energy, a new drive for accomplishment. Among those who had long supported the idea of suffrage there was no lack of confidence that women would live up to their new opportunity. In Baton Rouge the daughter of a former governor edited a weekly paper entitled *Woman's Enterprise* with the goal of proving to the world that women "are as fully alive to the demands of the times as are the sterner sex." The newspaper encouraged

1. Notes for a speech in Mary O. Cowper Papers, MS Dept., Duke.

women to register and vote, urged them to run for office, and issued constant reminders to officeholders that women now intended to be heard on all important issues. Women, the *Enterprise* thought, far from voting as their menfolk directed, were on the way to becoming the politically influential members of their families. "Place one energetic woman on a commission and a general house cleaning will result such as Baton Rouge has never enjoyed," the editors confidently asserted; "inefficiency in every department will disappear." [2]

In addition to politics the *Enterprise* carried a steady stream of articles on working women's problems, education for women, and the "new concept of marriage." It also directed a good deal of attention to the accomplishments of young women enrolled at the Louisiana State University.

For those who had taken it seriously the suffrage movement had been an excellent school in political methods. In the first flush of post-suffrage enthusiasm, the old hands undertook to try to teach the ways and means of political action to as many of the newly enfranchised as they could persuade to be interested. Even before the Nineteenth Amendment was ratified, state suffrage organizations transformed themselves into leagues of women voters, to educate women and work for "needed legislation." Charles Merriam, a well-known political scientist, was persuaded to offer an intensive training course for women leaders at the University of Chicago. "Citizenship schools" blossomed over the landscape, offering everything from the most serious reading in political theory to the simplest instruction in ballot marking. Meanwhile women established legislative councils

2. *Woman's Enterprise,* 22 July, 13 January 1922.

in a concerted effort to attain the laws they felt were
needed. The Alabama council, for example, was made up of
sixteen organizations ranging from the Woman's Trade
Union League to the Methodist Home Missionary Council.
In Texas the Joint Legislative Council published a carefully
compiled record of the work of congressmen, state legislators, and judges.

The central political concern had to do with the problems
of children. In nearly every state women were active in the
effort to secure better child labor laws. The case of Virginia
is instructive. In 1921 women's groups urged the legislature
to establish a Children's Code Commission, and when the
legislature took their suggestion, they persuaded the governor to appoint five of their number to the commission. When
the commission, in turn, brought in twenty-four recommendations for new laws, ranging from a statewide juvenile
court system to compulsory education, the women went to
work to secure legislative approval of the recommendations.
Eighteen of the twenty-four were adopted.[3]

Also in 1921 a combination of women's groups in Georgia
secured the passage of a children's code, a child-placement
bill, and a training school bill. In 1923 Georgia women tried,
but failed, to persuade the state legislature to ratify the
federal child labor amendment. In Arkansas, by contrast, a
woman member of the legislature, working in conjunction
with the members of the women's clubs, was given credit for
that state's ratifying the amendment. The wife of the man
who led the floor fight against ratification was reported to be
unable to conceal her delight that he had failed.[4] In other

3. Adele Clark Papers, Miss Clark, Richmond.
4. Mrs. E. B. Chamberlain to Mrs. Solon Jacobs, 25 October 1922, and
Report to Director of Southeastern Region, 10 January 1924, in League

states when women failed to secure ratification of the child labor amendment they turned their attention to strengthening state labor laws, an effort in which they were more successful.[5]

In 1921 southern women, along with women from over the nation, brought pressure upon the Congress to pass the Sheppard-Towner Act for maternal and infant health. Nineteen of 26 southern senators voted for the bill. In the House, 91 of the 279 votes in support of the bill came from the South and only 9 of 39 votes against it.[6] This law, which pioneered federal-state cooperation in welfare, was the first concrete national achievement of newly enfranchised women. Since the law provided for federal-state cooperative financing, it was necessary for the women to follow up their congressional efforts with work to secure the matching appropriations from state legislatures.[7] This campaign elicited a great deal of enthusiasm among women in every southern state. It was in those states particularly, where the machinery of public health was not well developed, that the favorable effects of the Act were most visible.

Next to children the subjects of most general interest to politically minded women had to do with the working condi-

___

of Women Voters Papers, Division of Manuscripts, Library of Congress, Georgia file; Alice Cordell to Marguerite Owen, 2 October 1924, Arkansas file. Referred to hereafter as LWV Papers, LC.

5. LWV Papers, LC, files of all southern states.

6. *Congressional Record,* 67th Cong., 1st sess., pp. 4216, 8036–37, 22 July, 19 November 1921.

7. This story is documented in detail in the LWV Papers, LC, state files. See especially the state-by-state reports on the operation of the law and the collection of letters from Texas women who had benefited from the maternal and child-care program instituted under the Sheppard-Towner Act. Reports of the Children's Bureau of the U.S. Department of Labor in the twenties also contain details of the actual workings of the law.

tions and wages of women workers. In Arkansas, for example, as early as 1919 the suffrage organization began to work for minimum wages and maximum hours in cotton mills. In Georgia women joined the Federation of Labor in an effort to secure a limit on hours of work for women. The hearing on this last measure brought out "every cotton mill man in Georgia," and while a woman's eloquent testimony persuaded the committee to report the bill, the millowners had enough influence to prevent its being brought to a vote. As a result of what they had learned about the conditions in which many factory women worked, clubwomen and the League of Women Voters developed a deepening concern for the problems of industrial labor generally. This concern often brought them into conflict with husbands and friends. The businessman's cherished "cheap labor" might be seen by his wife as an exploited human being, especially when the worker was a woman or a child. For years southern ladies had been praised for their superior sensitivity to human and personal problems, and now that their "sphere" was enlarging, such sensitivity took them in directions not always welcome to their husbands.

This particular drama of wives against husbands was played out, among other places, in North Carolina. Textile manufacturing was a major economic interest in that state, and working conditions in many mills were far from ideal. Wages were low, and it was common to find numbers of young children at work. Soon after the passage of the Nineteenth Amendment, North Carolina women began to develop an aggressive interest in these matters. It occurred to them to ask the state government to invite the Woman's Bureau of the United States Department of Labor to investigate working conditions in North Carolina mills. This suggestion aroused a strong opposition among millmen and their business colleagues. The governor was polite to the women but adamant: North Carolina had no need for the federal government to tell it how to run its affairs. Textile journals and newspapers accused the offending women of being unwomanly, of mixing in things about which they knew nothing, and of being the dupes of northern manufacturers bent on spoiling the competitive advantage which child labor and cheap female labor gave the South. The YWCA, one of the groups supporting the idea of a survey, was warned that it would soon find itself without funds. The state president of the League of Women Voters was summoned before a self-constituted panel of millmen and lectured severely. She was told that her husband's sales of mill machinery would diminish as long as she and the league continued their unseemly interest in working conditions in the mills.[8]

The progressive movement came fully into being in the South in the 1920s, especially in relation to state government. Southern women contributed significantly to the political effort which led to the adoption of a wide range of social legislation in those years. In public, women continued to defer to men, but in their private correspondence they described their own efforts as more practical than those of men.[9]

8. The story of the long fight between North Carolina women's organizations and textile manufacturers is covered in detail in correspondence in the Mary O. Cowper Papers, MS Dept., Duke. Mrs. Cowper was executive secretary of the North Carolina League of Women Voters. For a contemporary analysis by a sympathetic newspaperwoman, see Nell Battle Lewis, "The University of North Carolina Gets Its Orders," *Nation* 122 (3 February 1926): 114–15.

9. Successive issues of the *Journal of Social Forces,* which began to be published in Chapel Hill, N.C., in 1923 cover the growth in social

As time went by a small number of very respectable southern women became deeply involved in what could only be called, in the southern context, the radical aspect of the labor movement. Lucy Randolph Mason, whose name testified to her Virginia lineage, began by working with the YWCA in Richmond and became, as she said, more and more concerned about the lack of social control in the development of southern industry.[10] In her YWCA work she became acutely aware of industrial problems, for the young women in the Y, during the twenties, were preoccupied with the study of the facts of industrial life. They worked out a legislative program which included the abatement of poverty, abolition of child labor, a living wage in every industry, the eight-hour day, and protection of workers from the hardships of continued unemployment. At Randolph-Macon members of the Y studied the problems of coal miners, and at Westhampton those of unemployment. College girls across the South formed a committee for student industrial cooperation, seeking, as they put it, to Christianize the social order.[11]

In January 1923 the National Consumers League spon-

---

legislation in many states, and in some cases the names of the people involved. George Tindall, *Emergence of the New South* (Baton Rouge: Louisiana State University Press, 1968), chap. 7, is also to the point. Kate Burr Johnson and Nell Battle Lewis, "A Decade of Social Progress in North Carolina," *Journal of Social Forces* 1 (May 1923): 400–403 is helpful. Mrs. Johnson asserted in an interview with the author in 1963 that women were largely responsible for the fact that North Carolina was so progressive in the twenties. See also Jessie Daniel Ames Papers, SHC UNC, and Mary O. Cowper Papers, MS Dept., Duke.

10. Lucy R. Mason to Henry P. Kendall, 31 December 1930, L. R. Mason Papers, MS Dept., Duke.

11. Gladys Bryson, student secretary of the YWCA, to Lucy Somerville, 23 March 1923, Somerville-Howorth Papers, Schlesinger Library, Radcliffe College.

sored a conference on industrial legislation for the Mississippi Valley states. The session on hours of work for women was chaired by a New Orleans woman, and the one on minimum wages by a Kentucky woman. In the same year the chairman of the Women in Industry Committee of the Mississippi League of Women Voters urged members of local leagues to inform themselves about the working conditions of the 15,000 working women in Mississippi "in restaurants and shops, in bakeries and laundries and fisheries," about their inadequate wages, and their need for safety and sanitary protection. All this was to be in preparation for the next session of the Mississippi legislature.[12]

Middle-class southern women set up two schools for factory girls. One, sponsored by the YWCA at Lake Junaluska in North Carolina, offered what its founders called a brief social-religious education. Although the organizers of this school realized that political action to improve their wages and working conditions could not be accomplished by the working women alone, they felt that these summer conferences might stimulate girls to begin to study and think about their own problems.[13] The other experiment was the Southern Summer School for Women Workers in Industry, founded at Burnsville, North Carolina, in 1927. An outgrowth of the famous Bryn Mawr workers summer school, it offered training to factory girls many of whom, when the upsurge of unionization occurred in the 1930s, would become labor organizers.[14]

By 1931 the Southern Council on Women and Children in

12. Lucy Somerville, Report as Chairman of the Women in Industry Committee, 1923, Somerville-Howorth Papers.
13. Lucy P. Carner, "An Educational Opportunity for Industrial Girls," *Journal of Social Forces* 1 (September 1923): 612–13.
14. Alice M. Baldwin Papers, MS Dept., Duke.

Industry, made up of women, had been formed to work for shorter hours and to try to bring an end to night work in the textile industry. Lucy Mason worked for this group too, before she went on to her major effort in the 1930s as an organizer for the CIO.[15]

It is curious in view of the deep conservatism of the majority of southern women, many of whom never registered to vote, that those who did choose to live an active life were often found on the progressive side of the political spectrum. Part of the explanation is that the person who was bold enough to assume a role unusual for women was also likely to be radical on social questions generally. As the president of the Tennessee League of Women Voters remarked:

Some good souls are pleased to call our ideas socialistic. They are indeed uncomfortable often for some folk. Some timid souls of both sexes are only half converted to the new order . . . [yet] every clear thinking, right feeling and high minded man and woman should consecrate his best talents to the gradual reorganization of society, national and international.[16]

One evidence of the advanced thinking of many of the southern women who were most active in public life was the important part they played in what came to be called the interracial movement. Beginning in 1919, at a time when many Negroes were leaving the South and many others were coming home from the war with a new view of life, the interracial movement of the twenties was built on the foundation laid in the previous decades.

15. Lucy Randolph Mason Papers, MS Dept., Duke.
16. Report of the President, Tennessee League of Women Voters, January 1923, LWV Papers, LC, Tennessee file.

Southern Methodist women whose first tentative steps toward corporate concern with the problems of their Negro neighbors came in 1899, had established the Bureau of Social Service with Mrs. J. D. Hammond as its superintendent. Mrs. Hammond, whose husband later became president of Paine Institute, published a book in 1914 called *In Black and White* which laid out a program for ameliorating the conditions of southern Negroes. The book must be read in the context of its year of publication, and with the realization that the author was a southern woman whose parents had been slaveowners. Though she did not advocate social equality, Mrs. Hammond tackled nearly every hard problem which vexed race relations in the South. She announced that she did not believe Negroes to be inferior. In her cosmos, God had put black people on earth, as he had white people, to fulfill some destiny. In a series of hard-hitting chapters, she held a mirror to southern society which must have caused some soul-searching among such of her readers as did not throw the book away in disgust. Taking her stand firmly on the Christian ethic, she castigated her fellow white southerners for permitting Negro slums, for sending youngsters to jail whose home experience had prepared them for nothing but delinquency, for permitting inequity in the courts of law, for accepting stinking Jim Crow cars, for failing to educate talent when it came in a black skin, for not setting examples of honesty and fair dealing, for hypocrisy and insensitivity. *In Black and White* provided a blueprint for much of the work which developed in the twenties under the leadership of a group calling itself the Commission on Inter-racial Cooperation, headed by Will Alexander.[17]

17. Mrs. L. H. Hammond, *In Black and White* (New York: Fleming H. Revell Co., 1914).

In 1920 at a meeting of southern churchwomen in Memphis four Negro women came on invitation to speak of the needs of southern Negroes. One of them, Charlotte Hawkins Brown, head of a school for Negroes in North Carolina, told the gathering that she had been forcibly removed from a Pullman car on her way to the meeting. In the emotional stir of the moment the ninety-odd white churchwomen constituted themselves the Woman's Department of Will Alexander's Commission. The first head of this group was Mrs. Luke Johnson of Griffin, Georgia, under whose leadership interracial committees were organized in every southern state. Mrs. Johnson thought race was "one of the livest issues of the day and . . . a real test of Christianity and of citizenship." [18]

In Texas the women's interracial organization was put together by an energetic widow, businesswoman, and former suffrage worker, Jessie Daniel Ames. By 1924 women there were working to improve Negro housing, schools, libraries, to secure Negro farm agents to work with Negro farmers, for better health care, a school for delinquent girls, adequate railroad accommodations, and for textbooks dealing with the economic and racial development of the Negro people. They proposed an anti-lynching law which would have made every member of a mob liable to murder charges. The group also attempted to investigate particular problems of intimidation, and organized a speakers' bureau to take the discussion of race issues to the state. In North Carolina Mrs. Bertha Newell, superintendent of the Bureau of Christian Social Relations of the Women's Missionary Council of the

18. Mrs. Luke Johnson to Jessie Daniel Ames, 28 April 1924, J. D. Ames Papers, SHC UNC.

Methodist Church, and Clara Cox, a Friend from High Point, carried on the same kind of effort. In 1926 Mrs. Newell began working to secure better job opportunities for educated Negro girls.[19]

Women tried to deal with racial conflict and black problems in many ways. When the National League of Women Voters decided in 1924 to establish a committee on Negro problems with membership from every state that had more than 15 percent Negro population, women in eight southern states accepted appointment. Many of these same women served on local interracial committees, of which there were finally about eight hundred in the South. In Tennessee white women organized a special citizenship school for Negro women. Some individuals offered personal support to their Negro fellow citizens. Mary Cooke Branch Munford of Richmond made a room of her house permanently available to Negroes for public meetings, and a busy doctor's wife in Alabama waged a one-woman campaign for better Negro education. When the Richmond city council considered a segregation statute in 1929, it was Lucy Randolph Mason who, almost single-handedly, persuaded the council to defeat it.[20] In April 1924 the Mississippi Federation of Women's Clubs set up a committee on the condition of the colored people, and the president of the Colored Women's

19. Bertha Newell to Mrs. Luke Johnson, June 1926, J. D. Ames Papers, SHC UNC.

20. *Norfolk Journal and Guide,* 2 February 1929. See also Katherine DuPre Lumpkin, *The Making of a Southerner,* for the work of the YWCA before World War I and her own gradual awakening on the Negro question. The League of Women Voters Papers in the Library of Congress contain a good deal of information about league work among the Negro women.

Federation was invited to tell the white convention about the problems of Negro domestic workers.[21]

The most dramatic aspect of women's interracial work was the crusade against lynching, which began in the early twenties. A group of Georgia women sent a message to the *New York World:*

> We are convinced that if there is any one crime more dangerous than others, it is that crime which strikes at the roots of and undermines constituted authority, breaks all laws and restraints of civilization, substitutes mob violence and masked irresponsibility for established justice and deprives society of a sense of protection against barbarism.[22]

By 1930 under the leadership of Jessie Daniel Ames, who by that time had left Texas for Atlanta, the Association of Southern Women for the Prevention of Lynching took shape. At its peak this organization enrolled 40,000 small-town and rural churchwomen in an effort to bring to an end this most spectacularly disgraceful form of race conflict.

In the meantime southern white women inaugurated an increasing number of interracial meetings, in which there was fairly open discussion of the problems Negroes faced. Though Negro women leaders, for the most part, took care to eschew any demand for social equality, they did hammer away on such things as discrimination in the administration of justice, housing, Jim Crow cars, inferior education, and the need for the ballot. It seems likely that these efforts, ineffectual as they seemed in the face of the magnitude of the problem, nevertheless represented the opening wedge which would ultimately bring an end to the monolithic

21. Jessie Daniel Ames to Mrs. Luke Johnson, 24 April 1924, J. D. Ames Papers, SHC UNC.

22. *New York World,* 11 September 1921.

position of southerners on the issue of white supremacy. From slavery through Reconstruction and into the twentieth century, relationships between white and black women were quite unlike those common between white and black men, sharing as they did many concerns about children and home life across the color line. The fact that women were very active in the interracial movement is not surprising.[23]

In the twenties white women were speaking of their sympathy for Negro women who were, like themselves, mothers and homemakers. One point they made over and over was the need to protect the chastity of Negro women from the aggression of white men. Just as one antebellum woman had candidly remarked that she did not know whether her grandmother's sympathy for abolition stemmed from sympathy for slaves or for white women, so it might be wondered whether part of the concern for the chastity of Negro women was a reflection of the white women's distaste for the half-hidden miscegenation which existed in every southern community.

The interest of women in humanitarian causes had deep roots in traditional feminine philanthropy. However, the twenties also witnessed the beginning of some newer interests. As they studied the mechanics of government in order

23. There is as yet no adequate study of the racial concerns of southern white women, especially churchwomen, in the twentieth century. The story as I outline it here is pieced together from correspondence in the Jessie Daniel Ames papers, SHC UNC, and the Charlotte Hawkins Brown Papers in the Schlesinger Library, Radcliffe College. There is much more to be known, and a beginning could be based on the files of the Association of Southern Women for the Prevention of Lynching, which are at Atlanta University. For an assessment of the effectiveness of the association see John Shelton Reed, "An Evaluation of an Anti-Lynching Organization," *Social Problems* 16 (Fall 1968): 172–81.

to vote, women began to develop a concern for efficient organization. One of the tools for educating new voters to their responsibilities was the study of state and local government. As women went about looking at the way such governments actually operated they began to wonder whether they could be made more efficient. As early as 1922 women's groups in Virginia were working for improved election laws, and in the following year they undertook to learn about the executive budget. In 1924 the Virginia League of Women Voters concentrated upon tax administration, a subject which the controlling Democratic machine was not anxious to discuss. The same group successfully supported a bill to create a uniform fiscal year but failed in an effort to secure civil service, a conservation department, and reform of the county government and the state educational machinery.[24]

Such interests were not confined to Virginia. Women in Georgia and Tennessee became convinced that outmoded constitutions were the source of much inefficiency; and in both states campaigns for constitutional revisions were launched and eventually succeeded. Kentucky women in 1927 began to work for home rule for cities, improvements in local charters, and the adoption of city manager government.[25]

Women were interested not only in the structure of government; they wanted to make it more democratic. Their own long exclusion had made them sensitive to citizen participation. It was newly enfranchised women who invented the now commonplace idea of getting out the vote. In some

24. Nora Houston to Maud Wood Park, 12 December 1923, and later papers in LWV Papers, LC, Virginia file.
25. LWV Papers, LC, Georgia, Tennessee, and Kentucky files.

places their efforts led to spectacular increases. In Alabama, for example, 54.4 percent of the qualified voters voted in 1924 following a get-out-the-vote effort, compared to less than 30 percent in 1920. One county, where women had been particularly active, turned out 84.1 percent of its qualified voters.[26] Florida in the same year reported a 65.9 percent increase over 1920 in the number of voters going to the polls.[27]

The poll tax was a subject of twofold concern. Women's groups opposed the tax on principle, but as long as it remained in force, they set out to collect it in order to increase the number of qualified voters. In 1925 Louisiana women collected $30,000 to this end. The work of North Carolina women for the Australian ballot, which finally succeeded in 1929, was another example of an effort to improve democratic procedures.

Close to home, yet a long way from women's traditional concerns, were two other political issues that developed strength in southern women's groups in the twenties: government ownership of Muscle Shoals and the regulation of utility rates. Interest in both these questions resulted from studies of the cost of living. The movement that would lead to the Tennessee Valley Authority gained the enthusiastic support of women in Alabama and Tennessee. On these as on other questions politically active women took a pragmatic view without reference to traditional free enterprise arguments.

Interest in party politics antedated suffrage, and some

26. Report on the get-out-the-vote campaign, 29 November 1924, LWV Papers, LC, Alabama file.
27. Mrs. J. B. O'Hara to Ann Webster, 2 September 1924, LWV Papers, LC, Florida file.

women had long taken an interest in party fortunes. It had been the accepted doctrine that the national suffrage organization should be nonpartisan, since it hoped to get support from both parties for the national amendment. Individual women, however, had found it useful to work for one or another of the parties. Jane Addams tried to recruit Jean Gordon of Louisiana for the Progressive party in 1912 and Madeleine Breckinridge went on an extensive speaking tour for the Democrats in 1916. A keen interest in party methods and organization had been one of the by-products of the highly organized national suffrage campaign.[28] Carrie Chapman Catt, the commanding general of the final suffrage drive, was intent that women should find their way not just to the outskirts but to the center of power in the political parties. She said at the Victory Convention in Chicago in 1920:

The next battle is going to be inside the parties, and we are not going to stay outside and let all the reactionaries have their way on the inside! Within every party there is a struggle between progressive and reactionary elements. Candidates are a compromise between these extremes. You will be disillusioned, you will find yourselves in the political penumbra where most of the men are. They will be glad to see you, you will be flattered. But if you stay long enough you will discover a little denser thing which is the umbra of the political party—the people who are picking the candidates, doing the real work that you and the men sanction at the polls. You won't be welcome, but there is the place to go. You will see the

28. See Carrie Chapman Catt and Nettie Rogers Shuler, *Woman Suffrage and Politics: The Inner Story of the Suffrage Movement* (New York, 1924), and Maud Wood Park, *Front Door Lobby*, ed. Edna Lamprey Stantial.

real thing in the center with the door locked tight. You will have a hard fight before you get inside . . . but you must move right up to the center.[29]

A considerable number of southern women set out to follow this advice. Party organizations welcomed them, if not with enthusiasm at least with a realistic appreciation of their potential voting power. Some states began at once the custom that has since become standard of appointing a woman as vice-chairman of the state party committee. Many southern women showed an interest in running for elective office; and, though numerous obstacles lay between almost any woman and nomination, by 1930 only Louisiana had yet to have women in the state legislature. During the twenties women served as secretaries of state in Kentucky, Texas, and Louisiana, as clerks or deputy clerks of the Supreme Court in Georgia and Oklahoma, as commissioners of public welfare in North Carolina and Oklahoma, as commissioner of state lands in Arkansas, railroad commissioner in Florida, and superintendent of public instruction in Texas.[30]

One woman who made her way to the center of power was Mrs. Nellie Nugent Somerville of Greenville, Mississippi, who had been an active politician long before the Nineteenth Amendment. At the first election after it was legal to do so, in 1923, she ran for the state legislature, in a campaign that was a model of thorough organization, and was elected. She had been observing party organization long

29. Mary Gray Peck, *Carrie Chapman Catt: A Biography* (New York: H. W. Wilson, 1944), pp. 325–26.

30. Sophinisba Breckinridge, *Women in the Twentieth Century* (New York: McGraw-Hill, 1933), pp. 295–342.

enough to understand it rather well, and she hoped the newly enfranchised women would be similarly observant. She advised them to be certain they had a hand in choosing county committees and reminded them: "It now becomes the duty of women voters to take lively interests in the details of political machinery. When any meeting or election is ordered by your political party be sure you take part in it." [31]

The chief obstacle to women seeking power in the parties was the unwillingness of many male politicians to promote women of independent mind and political skill. They preferred more amenable females, and hence the forthright and well-trained suffrage veterans often found themselves at odds with the entrenched men.[32] Mrs. Somerville herself managed to surmount this obstacle, and in 1924 Mississippi Democrats were divided into a Somerville faction and a Percy faction, the latter headed by Senator Leroy Percy. At the showdown, the Somerville group won. Mrs. Somerville served as a member of the committee on permanent organization of the 1924 Democratic National Convention and marshaled supporters of William G. McAdoo in imposing array.[33] Her record in the legislature suggested that she understood the effective use of political power. When a bill she had initiated failed to pass, the fact was reported as news—as a rule anything she offered did pass—and her

31. Article in *Jackson* (Miss.) *Woman Voter,* 19 November 1923. For the details of Mrs. Somerville's campaign, see letters of her daughter, September 1923, in Somerville-Howorth Papers, Schlesinger Library, Radcliffe.

32. See the analysis of this problem made by the first woman vice-chairman of the Democratic National Committee, Emily Newell Blair, "Women in the Political Parties," *Annals of the American Academy of Political and Social Science* 143 (May 1929): 217–29.

33. Clippings and note in Somerville-Howorth Papers.

colleagues were frequently quoted in praise of her hard work and effectiveness as a lawmaker.[34]

Another politically minded woman who reached a position of genuine power in the party was Sue Shelton White of Tennessee, an independent court reporter, secretary to members of the Tennessee Supreme Court, and from 1920 to 1926 secretary to Senator Kenneth McKellar. In 1915 she drafted the first mother's pension law to be presented to the Tennessee legislature, which finally passed in 1920. She went from her job in Senator McKellar's office to practice law in Jackson, Tennessee, and was sufficiently effective in Democratic politics to be invited to work for the Democratic National Committee. With Nellie Davis (Tayloe) Ross she helped lay the groundwork for the extensive women's program of the party during the early Franklin D. Roosevelt years. A fellow lawyer, who was general counsel of the Federal Social Security Board, said at her death:

Sue knew politics from the inside and from the outside. Politics were more than a game to her, though I think she relished the intricacies of the game. She used her political acumen as an instrument for the promotion of the general welfare. And she wielded the instrument with a grace and effectiveness that delighted the wise and distressed the stupid.[35]

Mrs. Somerville and Miss White were exceptional rather than typical; few women were as effective politicians as these two. The overall picture of women's efforts to exercise real influence in the political parties, South or North, was

34. Ibid., clippings. She had the additional distinction of providing the state with another successful woman politician, her daughter Lucy, who followed her in the legislature in the 1930s and ultimately became a federal judge.

35. Jack Tate in Sue Shelton White Papers, Schlesinger Library, Radcliffe College Library.

not one to gladden Mrs. Catt's heart. Sue White analyzed the southern situation in 1928 in a letter to Mary Dewson of the Democratic National Committee:

> Women have been discouraged by the rank and file of the party organization. . . . We still have the old anti-suffrage attitude in the south, women have been indifferent, and their indifference has been preached to them, aided, abetted and encouraged. They have viewed politics as something they should stay away from. They have been told so and have believed it and the few feminists who have tried to push in have been slapped in the face. . . . And the few women who have been artificially reared up as leaders are not leaders of women and have been reared not to lead women but to fool them.[36]

Miss White's analysis was confirmed by Emily Newell Blair, the national vice-chairman of the Democratic party in the twenties. In Mrs. Blair's view, at the very beginning, competent women—the genuine leaders—had essayed party politics, but when they showed themselves unwilling to be rubber stamps they were replaced by women more willing to be led. These were the artificial leaders to whom Miss White referred.[37]

An increasing number of southern women undertook simple party work of the doorbell-ringing and envelope-stuffing variety—a trend that still continues. And whether they helped make policy or not, women voters believed they were affecting the outcome of elections. Women claimed to have defeated James E. Ferguson and elected William P. Hobby governor of Texas in 1920. In Mississippi Henry L. Whitfield, former president of Mississippi State College for

36. Sue Shelton White to Mary Dewson, 23 November 1928, ibid.
37. Blair, "Women in the Political Parties."

Women, was elected governor in 1923, largely through the efforts of alumnae of the college. South Carolina women thought they had a large hand in the defeat of Cole Blease. One South Carolina woman who worked through the whole campaign remarked innocently, "We made no partisan stand, we merely got out the vote." Tennessee Democrats, perhaps looking for a scapegoat, blamed women for the Republican victory in Tennessee in the 1920 election. The women themselves claimed credit for the return of Cordell Hull to Congress three years later.

In North Carolina in 1921 the federated women persuaded a reluctant governor to appoint their former president, Kate Burr Johnson, commissioner of charities and welfare. The legislature showed an equal reluctance to confirm the appointment, but, as Mrs. Johnson recalled it, "They were scared to death of what women with the vote might do, and one legislator was heard to remark, 'Well, we might as well put her in; she's pretty and won't give us any trouble.' " The forecast was inaccurate, since Mrs. Johnson, with the organized women behind her, became a prime mover in the struggle to secure a survey of working conditions in North Carolina mills, and by so doing soon stood high on the legislature's list of troublemakers.[38]

Evidence of the increasing effectiveness of women voters may be deduced from the vituperative attacks leveled against them. In addition to the suggestion that they were being used by northern manufacturers, they were accused of

38. These claims appear in letters and reports to the National Office of the League of Women Voters in the LWV Papers, LC. The information about Governor Whitfield is contained in a letter from Lucy Somerville Howorth to author, 5 February 1964. Mrs. Johnson's comment occurred during a personal interview in 1963. See also clippings in the Mary O. Cowper Papers, MS Dept., Duke.

being radical, unfeminine, of organizing Negro women, and of using "illegitimate pressure" to put across the measures of a "feminist bloc." David Clark, perhaps the South's bitterest enemy of child labor regulation, went so far as to claim that more babies died after the Sheppard-Towner Act was in operation than before. His *Textile Bulletin* attacked women harshly. The Associated Industries of Kentucky circulated a condemnation of "political women" reprinted from the *Dearborn* (Michigan) *Independent*. The *Louisville Herald* suggested the reason: "As we have said, the woman voter is making herself felt in ways not chartered for her. We will not go to the length of saying she is always welcome in these channels, but there are times when one may gauge the need for one's activity and curiosity by the ungracious manner of one's reception." [39]

Many of the women who undertook an active role in southern politics in the twenties encountered this ungracious reception. But their motivation was usually strong enough to sustain them. Those who had been trained during the two or three decades before suffrage, and who had been acutely aware of the disadvantage of being barred from the polls, were eager to move into a more active and effective political role in 1920. Their general goals had been worked out in the preceding decades. Their underlying motivation was complex, but at least two main drives were clear: first, the drive to assert themselves as individual human beings with minds and capacities that could be used; and, second, the drive to improve the world in which they lived. The balance of these motives varied from person to person. Some, like Lucy Mason, were primarily interested in social reform:

39. *Louisville Herald,* 9 May 1923.

When I was fourteen, a missionary's sermon made me want to be a missionary myself. Later I recognized that religion can be put to work right in one's own community. It was this belief that took me into the Equal Suffrage League, and later the League of Women Voters, both of which were interested in labor and social legislation.[40]

Others thoroughly enjoyed the game of politics and the feeling of power that occasionally accompanied it. Nearly all felt that significant reforms would be more easily achieved with women's help.

The Nineteenth Amendment changed a good many things, but it only partially modified southern culture. A number of difficulties remained in the way of women's full participation in public life. One major obstacle, in addition to the demands of home and family, was widespread male opposition, typified, perhaps, by the Texan who burned his wife's poll tax receipt to prevent her from voting. Equally important was the unwillingness of many women to assume and carry through large responsibilities. Often they had a vague desire to "do something" but needed leadership to find out what to do and how to do it, and there were never enough leaders to tap all the potential resources. A good example, no doubt an extreme one, was a Virginia town of which it was reported that when a certain Miss Terry was at home the town was alive with women's political activities but when she went to Europe all was quiet.

Around the handful of leaders there gathered a slowly growing number of supporters and workers, and when this

40. Lucy Randolph Mason, *To Win These Rights: A Personal Story of the CIO in the South* (New York: Harper & Bros., 1952), p. 4.

support was effectively channeled, specific goals were achieved. In almost every instance—as in child labor reform, for example—groups of men were working to the same ends, and frequently there was cooperation. Women's efforts were crucial in the areas of race relations and factory regulation. Through it all, the outward aspect of the southern lady continued to be maintained as the necessary precondition for securing a hearing. For some women, this was a perfectly compatible outward role, so long as their freedom of action was not seriously limited. Others impatiently called for an end to pedestals, but even they found it effective to operate within the ladylike tradition. The other side of the coin was that women were accused of not being proper southern ladies by those who objected to the substantive goals for which they were working, and who hoped thus to discredit the goals themselves.

No one would argue that the southern states became a progressive paradise in the twenties, but it is impossible to study the history of the welfare movements of the time without being surprised by the degree to which the spirit of progressivism was still alive, and the amount of hopeful optimism about the possibilities for reform that animated women in the face of the spirit of reaction which is often thought to have permeated the political life of the decade. George B. Tindall adumbrated the "business progressivism" of southern state governments in the twenties. To the picture he drew must now be added the decided growth through the decade of the conception of state responsibility for public welfare, not in the old custodial sense, but in the newer sense of ameliorating the underlying conditions that create serious human problems. To the growth of this idea and its application in law, southern women made a considerable contribution.[41]

In spite of all that can be shown to be true about the energy and initiative of newly enfranchised southern women, it is obvious that the high hopes and optimistic predictions of suffrage leaders were not fulfilled. The removal of legal and customary barriers to female participation in public affairs did not lead large numbers of women to assume civic or political responsibility. To a greater degree than many "new" women were willing to recognize, the traditional sphere was a comfortable and undemanding place. Perhaps human nature in either sex does not inevitably gravitate to situations of challenge, hard work, and responsibility. For the women who yearned for independence it was essential that barriers be modified, but for many others the new freedom was a marginal benefit, useful in the case of need (if one were widowed or never found a husband, for example) but not much valued otherwise. Women reform leaders learned that the great problem was to find followers who cared enough to work hard.

When all this is said, however, the fact remains that the post-suffrage burst of political and social effort created a milieu in which the emerging new woman could try her powers. Along with expanding opportunities for work, education, and associated activity, the franchise added another dimension to women's lives, and another option for women who wanted more than purely domestic experience.

41. Tindall, *Emergence of the New South,* chap. 7; Charles Pipkin, "Social Legislation," in W. T. Couch, ed., *Culture in the South* (Chapel Hill: University of North Carolina Press, 1934), discusses the overall accomplishments in social welfare in the southern states.

All are agreed that something
has happened to change the
status of women; some are very
happy over the change and
others are sad, tragically sad.

Edwin Mims,
The Advancing South,
1926

9

The New
Woman
Observed

From 1830 to 1930, a hundred years of far-reaching changes passed over the South, and to what effect, so far as women were concerned? It is difficult to assess the consequences of the new realities of work, political activity, education, religion, or self-image. The surface aspects of these changes can be measured with some precision, although even here the gaps are large. Every decade the census reported an increasing number of women at work for pay, but it told nothing about their reasons for working, whether they did so from necessity or choice, whether wage earning brought satisfaction or dismay, or how their husbands felt about working wives. There are statistics on marriage and divorce but they tell nothing about the inwardness of family life or the relationships of husbands and wives and children. The family, indeed, of all human institutions may be the most difficult to study historically because it is traditionally a private domain. We know that increasing numbers of girls went to college, but can only guess at what they brought away from the experience. Any summary which seeks to deal with the significance of these things must be impressionistic.

Hard as it is to get hold of, one must ask first about the family. It remained the center of most women's lives, and if women changed, family life was bound to be affected. Men and women, children and kinfolk, were parts of an intricate system; when any part of the system developed new patterns of behavior, all the other parts had to respond in some fashion. More than other Americans, perhaps, southerners had put their faith in the family as the central institution of society, faith that was slow to change. The South remained predominantly rural long after much of the nation had become urban and industrial. The strongly knit rural family with its widespreading kinship system was celebrated in southern memoirs and described in sociological journals well into the twentieth century.[1]

It was in the towns that the newer forms of family life first appeared as the old patriarchal mode began to give way to a more egalitarian way of doing things. Families were smaller, and more influenced by the outside world. Women and children who would once have been expected to bow entirely to the father's will were finding a voice. A woman born in the eighties could still remember that "no one ever questioned what Papa said," and Ellen Glasgow reported that her father never changed his mind or admitted he was wrong.[2] Theirs was the last generation for whom such memories were common.

Attitudes toward courtship and marriage began to reflect the changes in the status of women. Education and widening opportunities for work had diminished the desperate need to find a husband. A woman could wait for a man who suited her or she could choose not to marry at all, as many of the first generation of college graduates did. The relationship between men and women was subtly affected by the possibility that a woman could earn her own living. "Since we no longer need to marry for the loaves and fishes, woman being

1. Ben Robertson, *Red Hills and Cotton* (New York: Knopf, 1942), has some notable portraits of country women among his kin. See also William Alexander Percy, *Lanterns on the Levee* (New York: Knopf, 1941); John Donald Wade, "The Life and Death of Cousin Lucius," in Twelve Southerners, *I'll Take My Stand* (New York; Harper & Bros., 1930); Rupert Vance, "Regional Family Patterns: The Southern Family," *American Journal of Sociology* 58 (May 1948): 426–29.

2. Ellen Glasgow, *The Woman Within* (New York: Harcourt Brace, 1954), p. 70.

now amply able to support herself," argued the editors of *Woman's Enterprise* in the early twenties, ". . . marriage will straightway step upon a higher plane." They thought that woman's ability to support herself would protect her against becoming subservient after marriage and earn her more courteous treatment, while the woman who chose to remain single could be a self-respecting worker instead of "poor relation to a tribe of in-laws." It was also presumed that the working woman, if she did marry, would be "a more sympathetic, intelligent and companionable individual." [3]

Though women who made wifehood and motherhood the central purpose of life far outnumbered working women, club leaders, political activists, or professional women, the example of the minority nevertheless affected the home-bound. Hope Summerell Chamberlain married a college professor of patriarchal inclination and lived in Raleigh, North Carolina. She devoted the early years of her marriage wholly to home and children, and, since her husband did not believe women capable of managing money, she had to ask for every penny. All went well until her eldest daughter wanted to go to college and the father, predictably, responded that higher education was unnecessary for a girl. His indignant wife sold the only piece of family property which was her own and sent the girl to Bryn Mawr. The contretemps forced her to take a look at her own life, and her subservient relationship. After much thought she decided to continue faithfully to discharge her home duties but to shift her focus outward. There were many interesting things going on in the world around her, and she would now begin to take an active part in some of them. "It is an old

3. *Woman's Enterprise,* 22 July 1921; October 1922.

story," she concluded. "It has happened to so many besides myself." [4]

Such a candid description of the conflict of old and newer values was rare. It may be significant however that Ernest R. Groves, an early family sociologist who lived and worked in North Carolina, thought by 1929 that "only extremely isolated and traditional" women were entirely removed from the current of change and that nearly all women were voicing some desire for a larger role.[5]

In the South as elsewhere the number of divorces had been increasing more rapidly than the population since 1870. At first glance this seemed clear evidence of a growing social instability. A closer look raised some doubts about the soundness of this conclusion. For one thing, as William O'Neill has pointed out, while more marriages were broken by divorce than previously, fewer were broken by death, with the result that the proportion of all marriages which lasted a reasonable lifetime had been increasing. Even more important was the inner meaning of the increasing divorce rate. Did it mean that more women were strong enough to break an unhappy marriage? Ernest Groves observed that the authoritarian family of the patriarchal type effectively *concealed* discord. "The rapidity with which women have aged in the past, their invalidism, mental breakdown and early death have been in part because of the strain of concealing irritation that was not permitted self-expression." [6] One is reminded of all those self-sacrificing

4. "What's Done and Past," manuscript autobiography, MS Dept., Duke.

5. Ernest R. Groves and William F. Ogburn, *American Marriage and Family Relationships* (New York: H. Holt, 1928), p. 33.

6. Ernest R. Groves, "Some Suggestions for Treating Family Disorder by Social Workers," *Journal of Social Forces* 6 (4 June 1928): 573.

antebellum wives, and of the fact that Ellen Glasgow's mother suffered a mental breakdown, presumably because of her tyrannical husband. When women began to feel free to express discontent, and even aggression, the surface smoothness was certainly ruffled, but the sum of unhappiness may have been diminished.

While the South sometimes appeared to be the last stronghold of Victorian sexual attitudes, by the 1920s women both wrote and read increasingly explicit discussions of sex and married life. Frances Newman's ironical dictum that "in Georgia a woman was not supposed to know she was a virgin until she ceased to be one" was out of date when she wrote it. Newspapers devoted much space to discussions of the possibility that marriage as it had been known was obsolete, and Judge Ben Lindsey's proposal for a new style of companionate marriage was described without horror. A woman columnist announced to the world that one result of woman's emancipation would be an open denunciation of the double standard—and then proceeded openly to denounce it.[7] Even the old suppressed topic of miscegenation was more openly discussed. Slavery had been dead for more than half a century, but white men still crossed the color bar "to ease," one white man said, "in some measure the frustration that came to him through the code of conduct he himself had imposed upon his own womankind."[8] Whatever the complex reasons, there were enough such excursions to cause uneasy discussion and speculation as to their effects

7. Nell Battle Lewis, "Incidentally," *Raleigh News and Observer,* 26 April 1925. See also Dorothy Dix's columns in the *New Orleans Times-Picayune,* 19 February 1923 and passim; and discussions by Kathleen Norris in the same paper during the year 1923.

8. John Andrew Rice, *I Came Out of the Eighteenth Century,* p. 192.

upon family life and the personalities of southern white women.[9]

Few things were more important for changing the shape of women's lives in the family than the spreading knowledge of contraception and the general advances in medicine. While Margaret Sanger was still being harassed in her efforts to make birth control information available to poor women, the number of children in middle- and upper-class southern families was steadily diminishing. In 1840 it was estimated that there were 770 children under five for every thousand women between 20 and 44 in the urban areas of the South Atlantic states. By 1910 the number had dropped to 485 and in 1920 to 458. Though the proportion of children was higher in rural areas, even there it dropped significantly in eighty years.[10] Improvements in medical knowledge reduced the incidence of childhood illness and increased the life expectancy of mothers. Taken all together these changes wrought a revolution in the amount of time a woman spent bearing and raising children, and therefore in the strength and health available to her for other activities after the children were grown.

9. W. J. Cash, *The Mind of the South* (New York: Knopf, 1941), and Lillian Smith, *Killers of the Dream* (New York: W. W. Norton, 1949), each suggested that white men out of their guilt about passionate and unrestrained encounters with black women developed the theory that their own wives should be "pure," meaning non-erotic. Miss Smith thought wives had responded to this deprivation over the years with an unconscious effort to control the behavior of men and children so rigidly that everybody's psyche was out of joint, and hate and aggression rampant. While any student of the personal documents can think of cases which fit this theory, I suspect it is of limited application. The manuscript sources bear witness to many warm and, indeed, sensual marriages.

10. *Historical Statistics of the United States* (Washington: Government Printing Office, 1961), p. 24.

Women were inevitably influenced in behavior and expectation by the responses of men to new conditions. Groves noted that "it is rare for a man entering matrimony to understand how archaic and impossible the conventional thoughts of men with reference to the headship of the family have become," and certainly the most easily identified male response was that which wanted to hold fast to traditional relationships. The southern-born editor who refused even to read Ellen Glasgow's first manuscript and whose advice to her was to "stop writing and go back to the South and have some babies" was a type of southern man common in real life and in fiction.[11] There were other kinds, however. Not all men were frightened of the new woman. The editor of the *Raleigh News and Observer* and the chief justice of the North Carolina Supreme Court were far from being alone when they warmly and actively supported every measure which would widen opportunities for women. Some husbands took pride in the achievement of their wives and urged their daughters on to similar independence.[12]

Ernest Groves, whose wife was coauthor of several of his books, displayed an interesting ambivalence about emancipated women. In his book on the American family he spoke well of trained women, even of working wives, but his description of the problems such women created for their husbands seems to have been deeply felt. He suggested that the coming of the new woman had not yet led to a "corresponding reconstruction of the role of husband in the degree

11. Glasgow, *Woman Within,* p. 108.
12. See Desha Breckinridge's letters to and about his wife in the Breckenridge Family Papers, Division of Manuscripts, Library of Congress; letter from E. J. Woodhouse to the *Raleigh News and Observer,* 1925, and comments collected by suffrage women in *The History of Woman Suffrage,* vol. 6.

necessary to bring into accord the man and woman." [13] He thought one area of maladjustment was in the realm of sex. Once women had thought it enough to please their husbands; now they were being told, and beginning to believe, that they, too, had a right to sexual satisfaction. This expectation put a new burden on husbands and created new complexities when the woman did not find the satisfaction to which she now felt entitled in the bonds of a proper monogamous marriage.

Husbands were also aware of a certain social pressure, "since even the man who glories in his wife's outside successes is aware of the belittling remarks made about him and the common suspicion that he does not amount to much. . . . it is not strange if the unwilling male partner in a fifty-fifty marriage should become soured." [14]

Women, too, had to cope with social pressures. Whereas once it had been clear that no matter what her internal need for achievement might be, a woman had to satisfy it within the bounds of a decent domesticity, she now had some choice. She could remain single and become a professional worker, she could marry and enliven her life with volunteer work, she could marry and still hold a job, or she could marry and fit into the traditional pattern of domesticity. There is no way to compare the pain of having to choose against the pain of having no choice.

The new variety of options was not the only pressure. Women also had to cope with the rising interest in child study and the implication of a more complex and exacting parenthood. Child study groups multiplied in the South in

13. Groves and Ogburn, *American Marriage,* p. 33.
14. Ibid., p. 65.

the twenties, and earnest students of family life assured women that one road to fulfillment was to do a fine job of child raising. In the past when children turned out badly, it could be seen as the will of God or the working out of inherent human nature; now it could be attributed to the failure of the mother to know enough or practice enough of what she knew.

The importance of the image of the southern lady in the thinking of southerners, in influencing the behavior of both men and women, in shaping women's self-image, has been stressed throughout this book. What happened to the image by the 1920s? As might be expected of an influential idea so strongly held, which had once filled some important psychological need, the image of the lady was slow to die. As late as 1920 a southern historian, a suffragist, wrote an introduction to a set of biographical volumes detailing the accomplishments of members of the United Daughters of the Confederacy:

The Confederate woman. Imagination cannot dwell too tenderly upon a theme so inspiring. Reverence cannot linger too fondly at so pure an altar. The historian's pen, which tells of a Rome and of a Sparta—aye the pen of inspiration which tells of an Israel—has not portrayed her superior, if, indeed, her equal; nor may we expect to find it in all the hidden future. It took the civilization of an Old South to produce her—a civilization whose exquisite but fallen fabric now belongs to the Dust of dreams. But we have not lost the blood royal of the ancient line; and in the veins of an infant Southland still ripples the heroic strain. The Confederate woman, in her silent influence, in her eternal vigil, still abides. Her gentle spirit is the priceless heritage of her daughters. The old queen passes, but the young queen lives; and radiant, like the morning, on her brow, is Dixie's diadem.[15]

His words must have had an anachronistic flavor even as they came from the printing press.

Some idea of what was happening to the image of the lady may be gained from three novels, two published just before World War I and one thirteen years later. Ellen Glasgow's *Virginia* is about a proper southern lady, daughter of another proper southern lady, both of whom believed that the whole meaning of woman's life lay in sacrifice for husband and children. The book contains a rich gallery of female portraits, beginning on the first page with Miss Priscilla:

With the majority of maiden ladies left destitute in Dinwiddie after the war, she had turned naturally to teaching as the only nice and respectable occupation which required neither preparation of mind nor considerable outlay of money. The fact that she was the single surviving child of a gallant Confederate general, who, having distinguished himself and his descendants, fell at last in the Battle of Gettysburg, was sufficient recommendation of her abilities in the eyes of her fellow citizens. Had she chosen to paint portraits or to write poems, they would have rallied quite as loyally to her support.[16]

Virginia, the youthful heroine of the book, was just of marriageable age at its beginning, and she held firmly to "the romantic illusion that for *her* the world must hold wonders yet unseen." Miss Glasgow, of course, knew better, and showed it, in the sharply etched pictures of marriages in Dinwiddie. She touched on all the sorest points: the mulatto

15. Lucian Lamar Knight, Introduction to Mrs. Bryan Wells Collier, *Biographies of Representative Women of the South,* 6 vols. (n.p., n.d.).
16. Ellen Glasgow, *Virginia* (Garden City, N.Y.: Doubleday, 1913), p. 11.

child of the leading citizen, the inability of many southern men to appreciate a strong woman, the drunkard whose courageous wife kept a boardinghouse and never spoke of his inability to make a living. Few more biting criticisms of the image are in print.

Every girl born into the world was destined for a heritage of love or barrenness—yet she was forbidden to exert herself either to invite the one or to avoid the other. For, in spite of the fiery splendor of Southern womanhood during the war years, to be feminine, in the eyes of the period, was to be morally passive. . . . Was that a woman's life, after all? Never to be able to go out and fight for what one wanted!

.   .   .   .

It was characteristic of her—and indeed of most women of her generation—that she would have endured martyrdom in support of the consecrated doctrine of her inferiority to man.[17]

It was taken for granted that the husband would have many interests; the wife but one—him. The result was that "as a wife Virginia was perfect; as a mental companion she barely existed at all. She was, he had come to recognize, profoundly indifferent to the actual world."[18] So Virginia put her whole energy into making her husband's life comfortable and spoiling her children. The children grew up and left her, and the husband fell in love with a buoyant new woman, leaving his wife to live out her life in the dust and ashes of her image of southern womanhood.

If Miss Glasgow began writing of southern ladies with irony and ended writing with compassion, her friend Mary Johnston showed no such ambivalence. The heroine of *Hagar* was an unabashed new woman from the age of

17. Ibid., pp. 148–49, 152, 200.
18. Ibid., p. 307.

twelve, and all the typically southern ladies in the book came off very badly indeed. From Serena, the maiden aunt who painted china, to Mrs. LeGrand, the gentlewoman in reduced circumstances who assiduously protected her boarding-school girls from any contact with real life, Mary Johnston obviously found them all trying. They were foils for Hagar, who from childhood questioned the cultural tradition, rejected the protective custody in which her grandparents wanted to keep her, and became an independent woman writer. At the very end of the book she found a man strong enough to marry her.

Frances Newman's *The Hardboiled Virgin,* published in 1926, might be read as a kind of minor Don Quixote, a satire designed to provide the coup de grace to an outworn tradition. Miss Newman's heroine was, in the author's words, "a girl who began by believing everything her family and teachers said to her, and ended by disbelieving most of those things, but by finding that she couldn't keep herself from behaving as if she still believed them . . . a girl who was born and bred to be a southern lady, and whose mind could never triumph over the ideas she was presumably born with, and the ideas she had undoubtedly been taught." [19] The whole book is an ironical treatment of the attempt of an upper middle-class family to impose the southern lady image on a bright girl who, as she grew up, was exposed to one experience after another which her southern lady upbringing had not prepared her to handle.

In 1938 Ellen Glasgow wrote about *Virginia:* "It seems amazing to me when I reflect that so short a time ago as the second decade of the twentieth century, when I was working

19. *Frances Newman's Letters,* ed. Hansell Baugh (New York: Horace Liveright, 1929), p. 30.

from life on this portrait, the Southern Lady had not entirely disappeared from her once familiar surroundings." [20] In 1925 a North Carolina woman thought the image of the lady died when the suffrage amendment was passed.

Ah well,—the world will move, be the Confederacy ever so gallant! Tennessee, the iconoclast, has broken the idol. . . . The pedestal has crashed. There are many even now who would patch the idol together. . . . it is broken thank God, beyond repair. For . . . it was only an image after all. . . . In its place is a woman of flesh and blood, not a queen, or a saint, nor a symbol, but a human being with human faults and human virtues, a woman still only slowly rising to full stature, but with the sun of freedom on her face. [21]

Even though Miss Glasgow and Miss Lewis thought the southern lady gone forever in the twenties and thirties, the image had not entirely disappeared. It lived on, not as a complete prescription for woman's life but as a style which as often as not was a façade to ward off criticism of unladylike independence or to please men. It gave an illusory uniformity to the southern female personality. In fact, many varieties of women were visible in the new southern culture which had once allowed only domestic talents to blossom. Economic independence, education, and professional opportunity gave the chance for many kinds of development. Even so, the outward forms of ladylike behavior were carefully maintained. A woman lawyer in New Orleans, the founder of Negro kindergartens in Atlanta, and Virginia's most indefatigable crusader for education were

20. Ellen Glasgow, *A Certain Measure* (New York: Harcourt, Brace, 1938), p. 78.
21. Nell Battle Lewis, "Incidentally," *Raleigh News and Observer,* 3 May 1925.

each insistently described as charmingly feminine. A description of one of them in a Louisiana paper was typical: "a splendid example of a southern lady . . . charmingly feminine and attractive . . . although her success in her profession shows her keen mind and clearcut, forceful intellect." [22]

But if the image lived on as habit or useful protective coloration, if it survived in the fantasies of a few elderly men and women, it had largely lost its force as a blueprint for woman's life. What took its place? Where did southern girls growing up in the twenties find a model? No longer, as in the 1830s, was there a single prescription upon which all right-thinking people could agree. A young woman of 1925 had before her eyes plenty of old fashioned homemakers, busy with their beaten biscuits, fanning themselves on front porches on hot summer evenings. But the front porch was no longer the limit of woman's sphere. She could also see businesswomen, political activists, teachers and social workers, librarians and newspaperwomen, lawyers and doctors. The daily paper introduced her to active women not only in the South but around the country; the League of Women Voters urged her to take full advantage of the right to vote; from some quarters she was encouraged to go to college; the *Ladies Home Journal* invited her to think of combining marriage with a career. While her mother might emphasize the value of a soft voice and a disdain for alcohol and tobacco, she could also hear praise of the flapper as a type of woman "frank, free, vital and most wondrous wise . . . [of] wholesomeness and promise." [23]

22. Clipping in Judith Hyams Douglas Papers, Dept. of Archives, LSU.
23. Lewis, "Incidentally," *Raleigh News and Observer,* 22 November 1921.

It was generally taken for granted that she would work for wages before she was married. In Raleigh it was said to be quite useless to plan social events in the daytime, since all the young socialites had jobs. Nell Battle Lewis told her audience that in the Ideal Republic every woman who was not taken up with family, as well as the exceptionally gifted who could do two things at once, would as a matter. of course have a career. The idle woman, she said would be completely extinct. "The woman who does not work is missing one of the greatest lessons in life. Because of piti-fully false pride or indolence she is voluntarily foregoing one of the real joys of living." [24]

Increasingly the young woman could see middle-class women working after they were married. Chase Going Woodhouse, a sociologist at the North Carolina College for Women, made a study of over five hundred married profes-sional women and found to her surprise that most of them said they worked because they wanted money. Mrs. Wood-house concluded that the old-style feminist was passing— but what she may have overlooked was that the old-style feminist had found economic dependence galling. In any case it may have seemed easier and more acceptable to say that one needed money than to admit to aspiration for a career.[25]

Difficult though it is to measure precisely what had hap-pened to women and to their place in the society there can be no doubt that the changes taken together added up to a development of the first importance. It is evident that to

24. "Incidentally," *Raleigh News and Observer,* 24 June 1926.
25. Chase Going Woodhouse, "Married Women in Business and the Profession," *Annals of the American Academy of Political and Social Science,* vol. 143 (May 1929).

some extent the change in woman's role, in her work and self-assessment, had its own inner dynamic, a psychological and ideological dynamic. Turn-of-the-century emancipated women were fond of seeing themselves as the inevitable result of evolution. It must be clear, however, that no such major development comes about in isolation, and the very fluidity brought about by the immense social changes of the nineteenth and twentieth centuries, the breaking up of old ways of doing almost everything, created a climate in which the restructuring of woman's role could more easily take place.

It would be possible to argue that many of the changes traced here were the direct consequences of industrialization. As work, and husbands, moved out of the home, women were destined to become discontented and eventually to work out a new pattern of usefulness for themselves. The growth of towns and cities which was accelerated by industrial development also had marked consequences for women. The image of the southern lady had been created as part of the ideology of the plantation way of life; when plantations broke up and people began to move to town, the image as a real force in women's lives was doomed. This argument is an oversimplification, but it is clear that the majority of the women who fill the pages of the second part of this book were town-dwellers. Even prosperous country women were still exceedingly busy with the related chores of house and farm, and the far greater number of poor farmers' wives were so burdened as to be quite out of the mainstream of modern life. The town, by contrast, provided servants, leisure, the stimulation of group activity—in short, the essential milieu in which the new woman could develop.

Communication was also vital. A handful of antebellum women read English and northern journals, and many of them read books, but for the most part theirs was a world in which ideas moved slowly. The rise of the popular press and cheap magazines, the adoption of rural free delivery of mail, and finally the invention of the radio and the motion picture changed all that. Travel was increasingly easier. To the horror and sorrow of many southerners, Yankee ideas of all kinds came South and were domesticated.[26]

The common thread running through most of the changes a century had wrought was a movement from simplicity to complexity. Southern society itself had become more complex: people lived in a wider variety of styles, earned their living in many more ways, and were subjected to more diverse influences in 1930 than had been true in 1830. So it was that styles of women were more varied, their possible life patterns more numerous. By 1930 the culture permitted more diversity in female roles than had the antebellum culture. This meant that the potentialities of any one woman had a better chance of being developed and that the prevailing self-image of southern women was likely to contain new elements of self-confidence and independence. The evidence suggests that with notable exceptions, man's image of woman changed more slowly than women's view of themselves, a gap which could be a source of tension in family life.

A visible result of all these changes was that women began to affect the public life of society. If we believe the legends, every antebellum lady was a shining inspiration to her family, a model to her children, and an influence in her

26. Twelve Southerners, *I'll Take My Stand,* is the classic statement of the rearguard.

church and the community. Such influence, of course, was hard to measure. By 1930 women, singly and in groups, were taking a hand in efforts to change the way society conducted its most vital affairs. By insisting that child labor was immoral and that women workers needed protection, to choose one example, women perceptibly affected the economy of the region. They were emerging as a force politicians had to reckon with.

Not all southern women, to be sure, took advantage of their new freedom. A critical young woman scholar looked about her in 1925 and remarked with some bitterness: "Unless she is a woman of more than ordinary ability and energy she will elect to do what all her neighbors are doing: bridge, tea and gossip. In an attempt to busy themselves women have built a complicated system of social rank to which they have become slaves." [27]

For a complete picture the frivolous and useless must be taken into account—as must many other types ranging from some of the most effective political leaders the South produced in the twenties to the poor and often illiterate country woman, white or black, or the woman Frances Newman saw elaborately wasting time at the Piedmont Driving Club. The South had its share of daring young flappers, living side by side with devout, retiring churchwomen who would have been quite at home in the 1830s. All these women could hardly be said to have much in common; yet as a consequence of a century of change there was this: for the woman who had the capacity, the health and energy and fortitude, to seize opportunity, the culture now provided not one pattern but many. Few might take advantage of the multi-

27. Guion G. Johnson, "Feminism and Economic Independence of Women," *Journal of Social Forces* 3 (4 May 1925): p. 612.

ple options, but the options were there and would continue
to multiply. Southern women had begun to shake loose from
the tyranny of a single monolithic image of woman and were
now free, for better or worse, to struggle to be themselves.

Bibliographical Essay

The footnotes taken together make up a complete bibliography of the sources upon which this book is directly based, and there is no point in repeating them here. Those sources fall into several categories: manuscript personal documents, printed personal documents, biographies, contemporary commentary, a few works of fiction, and a handful of scholarly articles and books. What I propose to do here is to identify as well as I am able the origin of my general framework, and to point out, for other scholars who might decide to pick up some threads of this study for further investigation, the kinds of material I have found most rewarding.

My view of southern culture was shaped in the beginning by the fact of being born in middle Georgia and raised in north Georgia on the border between the low country and the Piedmont, by parents descended from either side of that significant antebellum divide. My father, an agricultural economist, was curious about social history, and his speculations formed part of the pervasive atmosphere of my childhood. Like the fish who has to be landed to perceive water, I became seriously aware of southern history only at Harvard, away from the South. Thereafter my perceptions were influenced by the works of U. B. Phillips, C. Vann Woodward, David Potter, Charles Sydnor, Clement Eaton, Kenneth Stampp, Oscar Handlin, and, among my contemporaries, George Tindall, Willie Lee Rose, and Eugene Genovese.

Once I began this study I discovered the important work of Julia Cherry Spruill, *Women's Life and Work in the Southern Colonies* (Chapel Hill: University of North Carolina Press, 1938), and Guion Johnson, *Ante-Bellum North Carolina* (Chapel Hill: University of North Carolina Press, 1937). While I was in midstream William R. Taylor's *Cavalier and Yankee* (New York: Braziller, 1963) appeared and provided reinforcement for my conviction that something had indeed been stirring among antebellum southern women.

Not directly apropos, but important in helping me think about these problems were Walter Houghton's *Victorian Frame of Mind* (New Haven: Yale University Press, 1937), Emily James Putnam's *The Lady* (New York: G. P. Putnam's Sons, 1910), and Doris Mary Stenton's *The Englishwoman in History* (London: Allen & Unwin, 1957).

Manuscript sources for a study of southern women are vast and have hardly been touched for this purpose. My own work was primarily conducted in the collections of the University of North Carolina, Duke, Louisiana State University, Tulane, the University of Georgia, and the Schlesin-

ger Library at Radcliffe. I am convinced that there is un-
mined gold in nearly every southern state. Even in those
collections where I have worked for a decade there is still
material waiting for examination.

Printed sources are also vast. The two compendiums, *The
History of Woman Suffrage,* edited by Susan B. Anthony,
Elizabeth Cady Stanton, and Ida Husted Harper (6 vols.;
Rochester and New York, 1881–1922), and Mrs. J. C. Croly's *The History of the Woman's Club Movement in America* (New York: H. G. Allen, 1898) constitute a mine of
data. There is also a great quantity of periodical literature,
from the *Southern Literary Messenger,* published at Richmond from 1834 to 1864, to the *Nation* magazine, which
devoted many pages to women, southern women among
them, in the 1920s. My footnotes give some indication of the
kinds of magazines which bear examination.

Memoirs and autobiographies present their own challenge. Numbers of southern women felt moved, toward the
end of the nineteenth century, to record for their grand-
children the world they felt had passed forever. Many others in those years published their wartime diaries. The
United Daughters of the Confederacy collected much useful
material. A few significant biographies of southern women
are in print; many more cry out to be written. An important
one not cited elsewhere in this volume is Sophonisba P.
Breckinridge, *Madeline McDowell Breckinridge, a Leader
in the New South* (Chicago: University of Chicago Press,
1921). Edward James, editor of *Notable American Women,*
was of immense help to me, and when his volumes are
available they should give an impetus to the study of southern women. A much earlier effort along the same line,
Frances Willard and Mary A. Livermore, *American Woman*

(2 vols; New York, 1897), is a storehouse of suggestive data about nineteenth-century women.

For the more recent period, published records of organizations such as the Woman's Christian Temperance Union are useful, and the manuscript collection of the League of Women Voters in the Library of Congress is indispensable.

Unlike the manuscript and contemporary printed sources, scholarly publications and unpublished papers bearing on this subject are so few that I can list a high proportion of the total. Hugh C. Bailey and William Pratt Dale, "Missus Alone in de 'Big House,' " *Alabama Review*, January 1955, is a fairly graphic account of a woman left alone to supervise a plantation. Eleanor Boatwright, "The Political and Civil Status of Women in Georgia, 1783–1860," *Georgia Historical Quarterly*, vol. 25 (December 1941), is exactly what the title suggests. Mrs. I. M. E. Blandin, *History of Higher Education of Women in the South prior to 1860* (New York: Neal Publishing Co., 1909) is a useful account. Elizabeth Davidson, *Child Labor Legislation in the Southern Textile States* (Chapel Hill: University of North Carolina Press, 1939), deals in part with the women's organizations working for reform. Marie Fletcher, "The Southern Heroine in the Fiction of Representative Southern Women Writers," a 1963 Louisiana State University dissertation, treats the changing character of heroines, and Francis P. Gaines, *The Southern Plantation* (New York, 1925), comes at the subject of this book by way of literature. Chapter 6 of Douglas Southall Freeman's *The South to Posterity: An Introduction to the Writings of Confederate History* (New York: Charles Scribner's Sons, 1939), called "The War through Women's Eyes," is very perceptive. Margaret Evelyn Gardener, "Sophie Bell Wright, 1866–1912," a 1959 master's thesis at L.S.U., deals with the life of one remarkable New Orleans woman. Marjorie Stratford Mendenhall treated "Southern Women of a Lost Generation" in the *South Atlantic Quarterly,* vol. 33 (1934) with insight. In 1945 Margaret Nell Price wrote a splendid master's essay, "The Development of Leadership by Southern Women through Clubs and Organizations." It is in the University of North Carolina Library. Kathryn Reinhart Schuler, in "Women in Public Affairs in Louisiana during Reconstruction," *Louisiana Historical Quarterly* 19 (July 1936): 668–750, summarizes her master's essay. The subject should be duplicated for other states. Francis Simkins and James W. Patton, *The Women of the Confederacy* (Richmond and New York: Garrett & Massie, 1936) was a pioneering work. Noreen Dean Tatum, *Crown of Service* (Nashville: Parthenon Press, 1960), the story of women's work in the Methodist Episcopal Church South from 1878 to 1940, has taught me a great deal. Elizabeth Taylor of Texas Woman's University is gradually writing the history of the southern suffrage movement. She has published numbers of books and articles on the particular state movements, most of which are cited in this book.

Finally there are the novels. In addition to those noted in footnotes and the three discussed in the final chapter, I have found the novels and short stories of Kate Chopin, recently reissued by the Louisiana State University Press, highly rewarding. So, too, all the novels of Ellen Glasgow.

The study of American women generally, and southern women in particular, has barely begun. Perhaps this outline of some of the sources will bring recruits to the task.

Index